THE
ESSENTIAL
Parakeet

Consulting Editor

BETSY SIKORA SIINO

Featuring Photographs by

RENÉE STOCKDALE

**HOWELL
BOOK
HOUSE**

Howell Book House

Published by Wiley Publishing, Inc., New York, NY

The Essential Parakeet is an abridged edition of *The Budgie: An Owner's Guide to a Happy Healthy Pet,* first published in 1997.

Library of Congress Cataloging-in-Publication Data
The essential parakeet/featuring photographs by Renée Stockdale.
    p. cm.
Abridged ed. of The budgie: an owner's guide to a happy healthy pet, first published in 1997—T.p. verso.
Includes index.
ISBN 0-87605-338-X
1. Budgerigar. I. Howell Book House. II. Budgie.
SF473.B8E77 1998   98-16433
636.6'865—dc21   CIP

Manufactured in the United States of America
10 9

Series Directors: Dominique DeVito, Don Stevens
Series Assistant Director: Jennifer Liberts, Amanda Pisani
Editorial Assistant: Michele Matrisciani
Photography Editor: Sarah Storey
Book Design: Paul Costello
Photography: All photos by Renée Stockdale
Production Team: Chris Van Camp, Jenaffer Brandt, Linda Quigley

CONTENTS

The Perfect Parakeet

Before you decide to bring a parakeet into your life, ask yourself the following questions: Do you like animals? Do you have time to care for one properly? Can you have pets where you live? Can you live with a little mess (seed hulls, feathers and discarded food) in your home? Can you tolerate, and appreciate, a little noise (the amount made by one exuberant parakeet) as part of your daily routine?

WHY A BIRD?

If you've answered "yes" to the above questions, you're a good candidate for bird ownership. Now your next question might be "Why do I want a bird?" Here are some of the answers you might come up with:

Birds are relatively quiet pets. Unless you have a particularly vocal macaw or cockatoo, most birds aren't likely to annoy the neighbors the way a barking dog or a yowling cat can. In many rental situations, birds aren't even considered pets, which means you can keep them without having to surrender a sizable security deposit to your landlord.

The small size of most birds makes them good pets for today's smaller living spaces. Many of us today are living in apartments, mobile or manufactured homes and condominiums, which makes the ownership of large pets who need yards and lots of regular exercise awkward and inconvenient.

Birds may be easier to maintain than dogs and cats. It is generally agreed that the daily maintenance time a bird requires is less than what a dog or cat needs. There are only a cage and small bowls to clean, instead of bowls and a litter box for a cat or the whole yard in the case of a dog.

Birds interact well with their owners. Although a bird isn't as blindly loyal as the average dog, he isn't as aloof as some cats. As an added bonus, many birds can learn to whistle or talk, which is beyond the range of canine and feline ability, and many owners find this amusing or entertaining.

Birds require consistent, but not constant, attention. This can be a plus for today's busy single people and families. Although birds can't be ignored completely, they are content to entertain themselves for part of the day while their owners are busy elsewhere.

Finally, **birds are intelligent pets.** Whoever coined the phrase "birdbrain" didn't truly appreciate how smart some birds are. Some larger parrots have scored at levels comparable to chimpanzees, dolphins and preschool age children on intelligence tests.

Are you purchasing a parakeet on a whim because you're attracted to his bright colors? Are you rescuing a bird from his aggressive cagemates? Are you buying a bird you otherwise feel sorry for? Noble though some of these reasons are, none of them is a good reason for purchasing a pet bird. Birds purchased for their pretty colors may soon be ignored or neglected by owners whose attentions have been captured by another fancy, and small, timid birds may be hiding signs of illness that can be difficult and costly to cure and that can cause an owner much heartache in the process.

If you feel the urge to become a parakeet owner, and you've bought this book first, you're on the right track. Although this book describes the care of budgerigars, also known as budgies, Americans refer to these birds as parakeets. For scientific classification purposes, these birds are different. However, as a pet bird owner, you need not concern yourself with this distinction.

If you purchased this book along with your parakeet, this is also a good first step, or if you've picked up this book after having your bird for a few weeks or months, congratulations! You're on the road to responsible bird ownership.

Many people find birds appealing as pets due to the relatively low amount of maintenance they require.

3

PARAKEETS AND CHILDREN

If you plan to purchase a parakeet as a child's pet, be aware that children in the primary grades will need some help from their parents or from older siblings in caring

for their new pet. Children in the intermediate grades should be ready for the responsibility of bird ownership with limited parental supervision. Or, better yet, the bird can be a "family pet," with each family member taking responsibility for some aspect of the bird's care. Even the youngest family members can help out by selecting healthful foods for the bird on a trip to the market or picking out a safe, colorful toy at the bird store.

Parents need to remind children of the following when they're around birds:

1. Approach the cage quietly. Birds don't like to be surprised.

2. Talk softly to the bird. Don't scream or yell at him.

3. Don't shake or hit the cage.

4. Don't poke at the bird or his cage with your fingers, sticks, pencils or other items.

5. If you're allowed to take the bird out of his cage, handle him gently.

6. Don't take the bird outside. In unfamiliar surroundings (such as the outdoors), birds can become confused and fly away from their owners. Most are never recovered.

7. Respect the bird's need for quiet time.

Parakeets are indeed beautiful birds, but beauty is not reason enough to get a pet bird; make sure you're prepared to commit to the duties of bird ownership.

WHERE WILL YOU GET YOUR PARAKEET?

Parakeets can be purchased through several sources, including classified newspaper advertisements, bird shows and marts and pet stores. Let's look at each in a bit more detail.

Classified Advertisements

Classified ads are usually placed by private parties who want to place pets in new homes. If the advertiser offers young birds, he or she is likely to be a private breeder who wants to place a few birds in good homes.

Most pet parakeets can leave the breeder's home at around 6 weeks of age, and the time between 6 weeks and 3 months of age is considered by some to be the optimal time to teach a pet parakeet to talk and to do tricks. You can tell baby parakeets by the series of stripes that cover their heads and necks (the stripes remain on the backs of the birds' necks following the first molt). Young birds also have small, slightly elongated spots on their face masks, while adults have large, round spots. Youngsters also have large, dark eyes that give them particularly endearing looks, where adult birds have well-developed white irises. Baby parakeets may also have dark or slightly black beaks.

If you buy your bird from a private breeder, you will probably be shown only the birds that the breeder has for sale. Do not be offended or upset if you cannot see all the birds that the breeder keeps; some birds are more sensitive than others about the presence of strangers during breeding season, and those that are sensitive may destroy eggs or kill chicks when they're upset. Parakeets are less prone to this sensitivity than larger parrots, but a breeder may keep all of his or her nesting pairs in the same area. If, however, a breeder is willing to show you around his or her facility, consider it a special treat and an honor that few people enjoy.

Bird Shows and Marts

Bird shows and bird marts offer breeders and buyers an opportunity to get together to share a love for birds. Bird shows can provide prospective bird owners with the

Your parakeet will do best if you speak to him softly and handle him gently.

chance to see many different types of birds all in one place (usually far more than many pet shops would keep at a time), which can help you narrow your choices if you're undecided about which species to keep. At a bird show, you can watch to see which birds win consistently, then talk to the breeder of these birds after the show to see if he or she expects any chicks. (This is especially important if you decide to show parakeets, because you want to start with winning stock.)

A bird mart is a little different from a bird show. At a bird mart, various species of birds and a wide variety of bird-keeping supplies are

PARAKEET OWNER'S SHOPPING LIST

When you go to the pet supply store to pick out your bird's accessories, take a copy of this list along so you won't forget any of the important items your new pet will need to feel right at home!

- a cage

- uncovered food and water bowls (at least two sets of each for easier dish changing and cage cleaning)

- perches of varying diameters and materials

- a sturdy scrub brush to clean the perches

- food (a good-quality fresh seed mixture or a formulated diet, such as pellets or crumbles)

- a millet spray (most parakeets love this treat!)

- a powdered vitamin and mineral supplement to sprinkle on your pet's fresh foods

- a variety of safe, fun toys

- a cage cover (an old sheet or towel that is free of holes and ravels will serve this purpose nicely)

- a play gym to allow your parakeet time out of his cage and a place to exercise

offered for sale, so you can go and shop to your heart's content.

Pet Stores

Pet stores can be the ideal place to purchase a parakeet. You'll have to check with stores in your area to determine if they sell birds, and then you'll need to visit the store and make sure that it's clean and well kept. Walk around the store. Are the floors clean? Do the cages look and smell like they're cleaned regularly? Do the animals in the cages appear alert, well fed and healthy? Do the cages appear crowded, or do the animals inside have some room to move around?

Did someone greet you when you walked into the store? Is the store staff knowledgeable and friendly? Do they seem to care that you came in to shop? Remember that you will be visiting a pet store every week or two to purchase food, toys and other items for your parakeet, so you might want to select a store with friendly people behind the counter.

After you've determined that the store is clean and the employees are pleasant, find out if the staff tries to keep their birds healthy. Do they ask you to wash your hands with a mild disinfectant before and between handling their birds? If they do, don't balk at the request. This is for the health of the birds, and it indicates that the store is concerned about keeping its animals healthy. Buying a healthy bird is much more enjoyable than purchasing a pet with health problems, so don't be afraid to follow the rules in a caring store!

CHOOSING THE RIGHT PARAKEET

Look at the parakeets that are available for sale. If possible, sit down and watch them for awhile. Don't rush this important step. Do some of the birds seem bolder than the others? Consider those first, because you want a curious, active, robust pet, rather than a shy animal that hides in a corner. Are other parakeets sitting off by themselves, seeming to sleep while their cagemates play? Reject any birds that seem too quiet or too sleepy because these signs can indicate illness.

Remember that healthy birds spend their time doing four main

Young parakeets are distinguished by a series of stripes on the back of their heads and necks.

7

activities—eating, playing, defecating and sleeping. If you notice that a bird seems to want only to sleep, for example, reject that bird in favor of another whose routine seems more balanced.

If possible, let your parakeet choose you. Many pet stores display their parakeets in colony situations on play gyms, or a breeder may bring out a clutch of babies for you to look at. If one bird waddles right up to you and wants to play, or if one comes over to check you out and just seems to want to come home with you, that's the bird you want!

Male or Female?

You may be asking, "Should I get a male or a female parakeet?" Although males may make slightly better talkers, your best bet is to concentrate on finding a young, healthy bird and enjoying him for his full pet potential. If you have your heart set on an older bird,

males generally have blue ceres, while females' ceres are brownish. But don't try this sexing test on a young bird because cere color develops as a bird matures.

One or Two?

Another question you may have (especially if you have a busy schedule) is "Should I get one bird or two?" Single pet parakeets generally make more affectionate pets, because you and your family become the bird's substitute flock. But a pair of parakeets can be pretty entertaining as they chase each other around the cage and encourage each other into all sorts of avian mischief.

If you have one bird and bring a new one home, there is the possibility of territorial behavior on the part of the original bird. This territorial behavior can include bullying the newcomer and keeping him away from food and water dishes to the point that the new bird cannot eat or drink.

To avoid this problem, house the birds in separate cages until you can supervise their interactions. Let the birds out together on a neutral play gym and watch how they act with

SIGNS OF GOOD HEALTH

Here are some of the indicators of a healthy parakeet. Keep them in mind when selecting your pet.

- bright eyes
- a clean cere (the area above the bird's beak that covers his nares or nostrils)
- upright posture
- a full-chested appearance
- active movement around the cage
- clean legs and vent
- smooth feathers
- good appetite

8

each other. If they seem to get along, you can move their cages closer together so they can become accustomed to being close. Some birds will adjust to having other birds share their cages, while others prefer to remain alone in their cages with other birds close by.

By the same token, don't try to put a new parakeet into the cage of a bird you already own, and don't house parakeets with other small birds, such as finches, canaries, cockatiels or lovebirds. Parakeets may tend to bully finches and canaries, keeping them away from food and water bowls, while cockatiels and lovebirds may exhibit the same behavior toward parakeets.

To keep peace in your avian family, make sure every bird has his own cage, food and water bowls. Some parakeets will get along with other birds during supervised play-time on a play gym, while others will not.

BRINGING YOUR PARAKEET HOME

Quarantine

If you have other birds in your home, you will want to quarantine

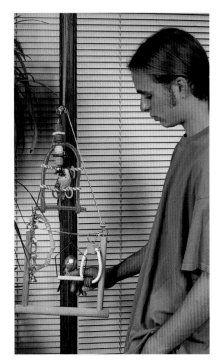

When choosing your parakeet, look for a curious and active individual.

your parakeet for at least thirty days to ensure he doesn't have any diseases that your other birds could catch. To do this, you will need to keep your parakeet as far away from your other birds as possible, preferably in a separate room. Feed your newly arrived parakeet after you feed your other birds, and be sure to wash your hands thoroughly before and after handling or playing with your new pet. Quarantine is usually just a precautionary

9

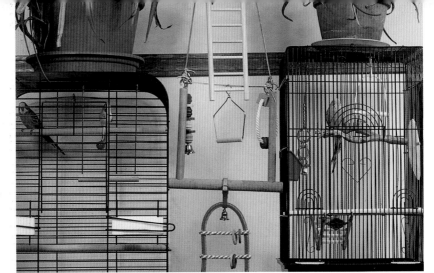

You may find that keeping two birds in one cage may lead to too much mischief and that it's more peaceful to keep them separately.

measure, but you can't be too careful when your pets' health is involved!

Adjustment Time

Although you will probably want to start playing with your new parakeet the minute you bring him home, please resist this temptation. Your new pet will need some time to adjust to his new environment, so be patient. Spend the time instead talking quietly to your new pet, and use his name frequently while you're talking. Move slowly around your parakeet for the

first few days to avoid startling him.

Your Parakeet's Routine

You will be able to tell when your new pet has settled into his routine and will learn to recognize his typical behavior. You may also notice that your bird fluffs or shakes his feathers to greet you, or that he chirps a greeting when you uncover his cage in the morning. If your parakeet should learn to talk, he may eventually greet you with a cheery "hello" or "good morning" as you uncover his cage.

Homecoming

Before you bring your feathered friend home, determine where she will live in your house or apartment. Selecting your parakeet's cage will be one of the most important decisions you will make for your pet, and where that cage will be located in your home is equally important. Don't wait until you bring your bird home to think this through. You'll want your new pet to settle into her surroundings right away, rather than adding to her stress by relocating her several times before selecting the right spot for the cage.

CHOOSING A CAGE

You will want your parakeet to have a good home. Some of the cages you'll look at while making your

Your parakeet's cage should be large enough to house your bird comfortably, along with her toys, perches and food dishes.

12

Size Is Important

When choosing your parakeet's cage, remember that it must be large enough to house your bird, her food and water bowls, perches and toys. *Bird Talk* columnist Susan Chamberlain recommends that parakeet owners "test cages for 60," which means that the measurements of the cage's length, width and height should total at least 60 when added together. A common size for parakeet cages is 18 inches wide, 18 inches high and 24 inches long, which adds up to 60. This would be about the smallest cage to consider if you own a single pet bird. If you have more than one bird or if your bird is an upwardly mobile creature with lots of belongings (toys, food dishes, a bathtub perhaps), a larger cage is in order.

Simply put, buy the largest cage you can afford, because you don't want your pet to feel cramped. Remember, too, that parakeets are like little airplanes, flying horizontally, rather than little helicopters that hover up and down. For this reason, long rectangular cages that offer horizontal space for short flights are preferred to high, narrow

selection are designed to sit on tabletops, while others have built-in or attached stands. Consider which will work best in your home. If yours is an active house with other pets and children, a tabletop cage may be better than a cage with a stand that could be knocked over. If you live alone in a small apartment, a cage and stand might be in order. If you do choose a cage with a stand, be sure the stand is steady and fits well with the cage.

cages that don't provide much flying room.

Acrylic or Wire?

Birdcages are traditionally made of wire, but you may see acrylic cages in magazine advertisements or at your local pet store. These cages are better at containing seed hulls, loose feathers and other debris your bird creates, which may make bird keeping easier and more enjoyable for you. This is a plus if you want to keep your home clean of birdie debris while still enjoying your pet birds.

Acrylic cages clean up easily with a damp towel and regular changing of the tray that slides under the cage itself. If you choose an acrylic cage for your pet, make sure it has numerous ventilation holes drilled in its walls to allow for adequate air circulation. Be particularly careful not to leave your parakeet in direct sunlight if you choose to house her in an acrylic cage, because these cages can get warm rather quickly.

If you choose a wire cage, examine it carefully before making your final selection. Make sure that the finish is not chipped, bubbled or peeling, because a curious parakeet may find the spot and continue removing the finish. This can cause a cage to look old and worn before its time, and some cages may start to rust without their protective

CAGE CONSIDERATIONS

Your parakeet will spend much of her time in her cage, so make this environment as stimulating, safe and comfortable as possible. Keep the following points in mind when choosing a good cage for your parakeet.

- Make sure the cage is big enough. The dimensions of the cage (height, length and depth) should add up to 60 for a single bird.

- An acrylic cage may mean easier cleanup for the bird owner. Wood or bamboo cages will be quickly destroyed by an eager parakeet's beak.

- Make sure the cage door opens easily and stays securely open and closed. Avoid "guillotine-style" doors.

- The cage tray should be regularly shaped and easy to slide in and out. There should be a grille covering the cage floor so you can change the substrate without worrying about the bird's escape.

13

14

finishes. Finally, if your parakeet ingests any of the finish, she could become ill.

Reject any cages that have sharp interior wires or wide bar spacing. (Recommended bar spacing for parakeets is between $3/8$ and $7/16$ inch.) Make sure the cage you choose has some horizontal bars in it so your parakeet will be able to climb the cage walls easier if she wants to exercise.

Cage Door Options

Once you've checked the bar spacing and the overall cage quality, your next concern should be the cage door. Does it open easily for you, yet remain secure enough to keep your bird in her cage when you close the door? Is it wide enough for you to

get your hand in and out of the cage comfortably? Will your bird's food bowl or a bowl of bath water fit through it easily? Does the door open up, down or to the side? Some bird owners prefer that their pets have a play porch on a door that opens drawbridge style, while others are happy with doors that open to the side. Watch out for guillotine-style doors that slide up and over the cage entrance, because some parakeets have suffered broken legs when a door dropped on them unexpectedly.

Substrate

Next, look at the cage tray. Does it slide in and out of the cage easily? Remember that you will be changing the paper in this tray at least once a day for the rest of your bird's life (about fifteen years with good care). Is the tray an odd shape or size?

It is important to choose a suitable cage substrate (the lining of the cage tray). Clean black-and-white newsprint, paper towels or clean sheets of used computer printer paper are recommended substrates. Sand, ground corncobs or walnut shells may be sold by your pet supply store, but these materials tend to make owners lazy in their cage cleaning habits. They hide feces and discarded food quite well. This can cause a bird owner to forget to change the cage tray on the principle that if it doesn't look dirty, it must not be dirty.

On a related note, you may see sandpaper or "gravel paper" sold in some pet stores as a cage tray liner. This product is supposed to provide a parakeet with an opportunity to ingest grit, which is purported to help aid digestion by providing coarse grinding material that will help break up food in the bird's gizzard. However, this lining causes impacted crops, a serious condition that requires immediate veterinary attention. Additionally, if a bird stands on rough sandpaper when she's on the cage floor, she could become prone to infections and other foot problems from the rough surface of the paper. For your parakeet's health, please don't use these gravel-coated papers.

Cage Floor

Finally, check the floor of the cage you've chosen. Does it have a grille that will keep your bird out of the debris that falls to the bottom of the cage, such as feces, seed hulls, molted feathers and discarded food? To ensure your pet's long-term good health, it's best to have a grille between your curious pet and the remains of her day in the cage tray. Also, it's easier to keep your parakeet in her cage while you're cleaning the cage tray if there's a grille between the cage and the tray.

The Cage Cover

One important, but sometimes overlooked, accessory is the cage cover. Be sure that you have something to cover your parakeet's cage with when it's time to put your pet to bed each night. The act of covering the cage seems to calm many pet birds and convince them that it's really time to go to bed although they may hear the sounds of an active family evening in the background.

You can purchase a cage cover, or you can use an old sheet, blanket or towel that is clean and free of holes. Be aware that some birds like to chew on their cage covers through the cage bars. If your bird does this, replace the cover when it becomes too holey to do its job effectively. Replacing a well-chewed cover will also help keep your bird from becoming entangled in the cover or caught in a ragged clump of threads.

CAGE LOCATION

Now that you've picked the perfect cage for your pet, where will you put it in your home? Your parakeet will be happiest when she can feel like she's part of the family, so the living room, family room or dining room may be among the best places for your bird. If your parakeet is a child's pet, she may do well living in her young owner's room. (Parents should still check on the parakeet daily, though, to ensure that she's being fed and watered and that her cage is clean.) Whatever room you choose, keep the cage out of direct

sunlight, and make sure that the cage is placed up against a solid wall so that your parakeet doesn't become stressed by feeling that her home is exposed on all sides.

Avoid keeping your parakeet in the bathroom or kitchen, because sudden temperature fluctuations or fumes from cleaning products used in those rooms could harm your pet. Another spot to avoid is a busy hall or entryway, because the activity level in these spots may be too much for your bird.

ADDITIONAL SUPPLIES

Along with the perfect-sized cage in the ideal location in your home, your pet will need a few cage accessories. These include food and water dishes, perches and toys.

Food and Water Dishes

When selecting dishes for your parakeet, be sure to pick up several sets so that mealtime cleanups are quick and easy. Choose only uncovered dishes for your pet's food and water because parakeets are often reluctant to stick their heads into hooded feeders to eat. Some have even starved to death rather than eat from a covered dish. Be sure to check your bird's seed dish daily to make sure that she has seeds, rather than just empty seed hulls in the dish, and refill when necessary.

Perches

When choosing perches for your pet's cage, try to buy two different diameters or materials so your bird's feet won't get tired of standing on the same-sized perch of the same consistency day after day. Think of how tired your feet would feel if you stood on a piece of wood in your bare feet all day, then imagine how it would feel to stand barefoot on that piece of wood everyday for ten or fifteen years. Sounds pretty uncomfortable, doesn't it? That's basically what your bird has to look forward to if you don't vary her perching choices.

The recommended diameter for parakeet perches is $1/2$ inch, so try to buy one perch that is this size and one that is slightly larger ($5/8$ inch, for example) to give your pet a chance to stretch her foot muscles. Birds spend almost all of their lives standing, so keeping their feet

It's best to keep your parakeet's cage out of direct sunlight and out of reach of curious felines.

17

healthy is important. Also, avian foot problems, such as bumblefoot or pressure sores on the soles of the feet, are much easier to prevent than they are to treat.

When you walk down the bird-care aisle at your local pet store, you'll probably notice that a variety of perch materials are available to bird owners. Along with the traditional wooden dowels are manzanita branches, PVC tubes, rope perches, and terra-cotta or concrete grooming perches. Each has its advantages.

Manzanita offers birds varied diameters on the same perch, along with chewing possibilities, while PVC is pretty indestructible. (Make sure any PVC perches you offer your bird have been scuffed slightly with sandpaper to improve traction.) Rope perches also offer varied diameters and a softer perching surface than wood or plastic, and terra-cotta and concrete provide slightly abrasive surfaces that birds can use to groom their beaks without severely damaging the skin on their feet in the process. Some bird owners have reported that their pets have suffered foot abrasions with these perches, however; watch your parakeet carefully for signs of sore

feet (signs may include an inability to perch or climb, favoring a foot or raw, sore skin on the feet) if you choose to use these perches in your pet's cage. If your bird shows signs of lameness, remove the abrasive perches immediately and arrange for your avian veterinarian to examine your bird.

To further help your bird avoid foot problems, do not use sandpaper covers on her perches. These sleeves, touted as nail trimming devices, really do little to trim a parrot's nails because birds don't usually drag their nails along their perches. What the sandpaper perch covers are good at doing, though, is abrading the surface of your parakeet's feet, which can leave them vulnerable to infections and can make movement painful.

When placing perches in your parakeet's cage, try to vary the heights slightly so your bird can enjoy different levels in her cage. Don't place any perches over food or water dishes, because birds will contaminate food or water by defecating in it. Finally, place one perch higher than the rest for a nighttime sleeping roost. Parakeets and other parrots like to sleep on the highest

When purchasing food and water dishes for your parakeet, select dishes that are uncovered, not hooded.

point they can find to perch, so please provide this security for your pet.

Choosing the Right Toys

When selecting toys for your pet, keep a few safety tips in mind.

SIZE

First, is the toy the right size for your bird? Large toys can be intimidating to small birds, which makes the birds less likely to play with them. On the other end of the spectrum, larger parrots can easily destroy toys designed for smaller birds, and they can injure themselves severely in the process.

SAFETY

Is the toy safe? Good choices include sturdy wooden toys (either undyed or painted with bird-safe vegetable dye or food coloring), strung on closed-link chains or vegetable-tanned leather thongs, and rope toys. If you purchase rope toys for your parakeet, make sure her nails are trimmed regularly to prevent them from snagging in the rope, and discard the toy when it becomes frayed to prevent accidents.

Unsafe items to watch out for are brittle plastic toys that can be shattered into fragments easily by a parakeet's busy beak, lead-weighted toys that can be cracked open to expose the dangerous lead to curious birds, loose-link chains that can catch toenails or beaks, ring toys that are too small to climb through safely or jingle-type bells that can trap toes, tongues or beaks.

MIRRORS

Mirrors are found on many parakeet toys, and most birds are fascinated with and enamored of that handsome pet in the reflection. Some birds become so infatuated with "the other bird" that they seem

While a mirror toy may make for entertaining bird watching, your bird's new mirror buddy may cause your pet to lose interest in you.

to lose interest in their owners, so you might want to wait until your parakeet is settled in her surroundings and comfortable with you before adding a mirrored toy to her cage.

HOMEMADE TOYS

Some entertaining toys can be made at home. Give your parakeet an empty paper towel roll or toilet paper tube (from unscented paper only, please), string some Cheerios on a piece of vegetable-tanned leather or offer your bird a dish of uncooked pasta pieces to destroy.

When you're putting toys in your parakeet's cage for the first time, you might want to leave the toy next to the cage for a few days before actually putting it inside. Some birds accept new items in their cages almost immediately, but others need a few days to size up a new toy, dish or perch before sharing cage space with it.

Noise Company

If you leave your parakeet home alone for long periods of time, it is a good idea to leave on a radio or television. Although parakeets have been kept as pets for about 150 years, they may still instinctively harken back to their wild roots at times. Because you don't want a stressed-out pet (silence suggests a predator nearby), leave a radio or television on for your parakeet if you will be away so that she will have some background noise and some variety in her daily routine.

The Play Gym

Although your parakeet will spend quite a bit of time in her cage, she will also need time out of her cage to exercise and enjoy a change of scenery. A play gym can be just what your parakeet needs to keep her physically and mentally active.

If you visit a large pet store or bird specialty store, or look through the pages of any pet bird hobbyist magazine, you will see a variety of play gyms on display. You can choose a complicated gym with a series of ladders, swings, perches and toys, or you can purchase a simple T-stand that has a place for food and water bowls and an eyescrew or two from which you can hang toys.

Homemade toys, like these made from toilet paper rolls, can be as much fun for your parakeet as store-bought toys.

21

If you're really handy with tools, you can even construct a gym to your parakeet's size and playing specifications.

As with the cage, the location of your parakeet's play gym will be a consideration. You will want the gym placed in a secure location in your home that is safe from other curious pets, ceiling fans, open windows and other household hazards.

Better Parakeet Care

TEN STEPS TO BETTER BIRD CARE

Bird keeping isn't particularly difficult. In fact, if you only do ten things for your parakeet for as long as you own him, your bird will enjoy a pretty healthy, well-adjusted life.

First, provide an adequate cage in a safe, secure location in your home. The cage should be located in a fairly active part of your home so your bird will feel as if he's part of your family and your daily routine.

Next, clean the cage regularly to protect your pet from illness and to make his surroundings more enjoyable for both of you.

Third, clip your bird's wings regularly to ensure his safety. A bird that can fly can injure himself severely, as well as inadvertently escape. Also bird-proof your home and practice bird safety by closing windows and doors securely before you let your bird out of his cage.

Fourth, offer your parakeet a varied diet that includes seeds or pellets, fresh vegetables and fruits cut into parakeet-size portions and healthy people food, such as raw or cooked pasta and fresh or toasted whole-wheat bread.

Your parakeet should also have access to clean, fresh drinking water at all times.

Next, establish a good working relationship with a qualified avian veterinarian early on in your bird ownership. Don't wait for an emergency to locate a veterinarian.

Sixth, take your parakeet to the veterinarian for regular checkups, as well as when you notice a change in his routine. Preventive care helps head off serious problems before they develop.

Seventh, set and maintain a routine for your parakeet. Make sure that he's fed at about the same time each day, that he gets regular playtime out of his cage and that bedtime is well established.

Eighth, provide an interesting environment for your bird. Entertain and challenge your bird's curiosity with a variety of safe toys.

Ninth, leave a radio or television on for your bird when you are away from home, because a too-quiet environment can be stressful for many birds, and stress can cause illness or other problems for your pet.

Finally, pay attention to your parakeet on a consistent basis. Set aside a portion of each day to spend with your parakeet—you'll both enjoy it and your relationship will grow. Besides, wasn't companionship one of the things you were looking for when you picked your parakeet as a pet?

A ROUTINE FOR YOU AND YOUR PARAKEET

A parakeet requires a certain level of care every day to ensure his health and well-being. Birds are happiest when they are secure and comfortable in a safe environment. You can help your parakeet feel more secure by establishing a daily routine and performing the same rituals at around the same time every day. This way, your parakeet knows his needs will be met by the people he considers to be his family. Here are

23

HOLIDAY PRECAUTIONS

The holidays bring their own special set of stresses, and they can also be hazardous to your parakeet's health. Drafts from frequently opening and closing doors can have an impact on your bird's health, and the bustle of a steady stream of visitors can add to your pet's stress level (as well as your own).

Chewing on holiday plants, such as poinsettia, holly and mistletoe, can make your bird sick, as can chewing on tinsel or ornaments.

some of the things you'll need to do each day for your pet:

- Observe your pet for any changes in his routine (report any changes to your avian veterinarian immediately).

- Offer fresh food and remove old food. Wash the food dish thoroughly with detergent and water. Rinse thoroughly and allow to dry.

- Provide fresh water and remove the previous dish. Wash dish as above.

- Change the paper in the cage tray.

- Let the bird out of his cage for supervised playtime.

Finally, you'll want to cover your bird's cage at about the same time every night to indicate bedtime. Keep in mind that your pet will require eight to ten hours of sleep a day, but you can expect that he will take naps during the day to supplement his nightly snooze.

Be Alert to Health Indicators

Although it may seem a bit unpleasant to discuss, your bird's droppings require daily monitoring because they can tell you a lot about his general health. Parakeets will produce small, flat droppings that appear white in the center with a dark green edge. These droppings are usually composed of equal amounts of fecal material (the green edge), urine (the clear liquid portion) and urates (the white or cream-colored center). A healthy parakeet generally eliminates between twenty-five and fifty times a day, although your bird may go more or less often.

Texture and consistency, along with frequency or lack of droppings, can let you know how your pet is feeling.

The color of droppings can also provide an indication of health. Birds that have psittacosis typically have bright, lime-green droppings, while healthy birds have avocado or darker green and white droppings. Birds with liver problems may produce droppings that are yellowish or reddish; birds that have internal bleeding will produce dark, tarry droppings.

Note, however, that a color change doesn't necessarily indicate poor health. For example, birds that eat pelleted diets tend to have darker droppings than their seed-eating companions, while parrots that have splurged on a certain fresh food soon have droppings with that characteristic color. Birds that overdo sweet potatoes, blueberries or raspberries produce orange, blue or red droppings, respectively.

As part of your daily cage cleaning and observation of your feathered friend, look at his droppings carefully. Learn what is normal for your bird in terms of color, consistency and frequency, and report any changes to your avian veterinarian promptly.

Weekly Chores

Some of a parakeet owner's weekly chores will include:

- Removing old food from cage bars and from the corners of the cage where it invariably falls.

- Removing, scraping and replacing the perches to keep them clean and free of debris (you might also want to sand them lightly with coarse grain sandpaper to clean them further and improve perch traction for your pet).

- Rotating toys in your bird's cage to keep them interesting. Remember to discard any toys

Your parakeet will require eight to ten hours of sleep a day, and a sheet over his cage at night will help keep his schedule in sync with yours.

25

that show excessive signs of wear (frayed rope, cracked plastic or well-chewed wood).

You can simplify the weekly cage cleaning process by placing the cage in the shower and letting hot water from the shower head do some of the work. Be sure to remove your parakeet, his food and water dishes, the cage tray paper and his toys before putting the cage into the shower. You can let the hot water run over the cage for a few

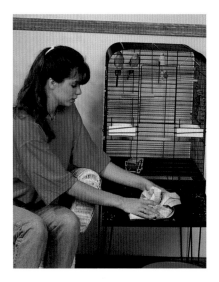

One of your daily chores will be replacing the newspaper in the bottom of your parakeet's cage.

26

debris, you can disinfect the cage with a spray-on disinfectant that you can purchase at your pet store. Make sure to choose a bird-safe product, and read the instructions fully before use.

Rinse the cage thoroughly and dry it completely before returning your bird and his accessories to the cage. (If you have wooden perches in the cage, you can dry them more quickly by placing the wet dowels in a 400-degree oven for 10 minutes. Let the perches cool before you put them back in the cage.)

minutes, then scrub any stuck-on food with an old toothbrush or some fine-grade steel wool. After you've removed the food and other

WARM WEATHER WARNING

On a warm day, you may notice your bird sitting with his wings held away from his body, rolling his tongue and holding his mouth open. This is how a bird cools itself off. Watch your bird carefully on warm days because he can overheat quickly and may suffer heatstroke, which requires veterinary care. If you live in a warm climate, ask your avian veterinarian how you can protect your bird from this potentially serious problem.

Seasonal Needs

Warm weather requires a little extra vigilance on your part to ensure that your pet remains comfortable. To help keep your parakeet cool, keep him out of direct sun, offer him lots of fresh, juicy vegetables and fruits (be sure to remove these fresh foods from the cage promptly to prevent your bird from eating spoiled food) and mist him lightly with a clean spray bottle (filled with water only) that is used solely for his showers.

By the same token, pay attention to your bird's needs when the weather turns cooler. You may want to use a heavier cage cover, especially if you lower the heat in your home at bedtime, or you may want to move the bird's cage to another location in your home that is warmer or less drafty.

TRAVELING WITH YOUR BIRD

The situation may arise when you want to take your pet on vacation or relocate him to another state or country with the rest of the family. If you are evaluating whether to leave the bird behind or whether to bring him along on your trip, you should ask yourself the following questions:

- Is there a trusted relative or friend that you can leave the bird with while you are away?

- Does your avian veterinarian's office offer boarding?

- How long will you be gone?

- Will you be visiting a foreign country?

If you are going on a family vacation, it is usually best to leave the bird at home in familiar surroundings with his own food, water and cage or in the care of a trusted friend, relative, pet sitter or avian

veterinarian. Birds are creatures of habit that like their routines, and taking birds across state lines or international boundaries is not without risk. Although it may be difficult to leave your bird behind, it is probably better for the bird to stay home.

Should you choose to leave your pet at home while you're away, you have several care options available to you. First, you can recruit the services of a trusted friend or relative, which is an inexpensive and convenient solution for many pet owners. You can return the pet-sitting favor when your friend or relative goes out of town.

27

During hot weather, your parakeet may benefit from a light misting with a spray bottle.

The first step in preventing a parakeet escape is making sure the cage door locks securely.

28

If your trusted friends and relatives live far away, you can hire a professional pet sitter (many advertise in the Yellow Pages, and some offer additional services, such as picking up mail, watering your plants and leaving lights and/or radios on to make your home look occupied while you're gone). If you're unsure about what to look for in a pet sitter, the National Association of Pet Sitters offers the following tips:

Arrange to have the pet sitter come to your home before you leave on your trip to meet the pets and discuss what services you would like him or her to perform while you're away. During the initial interview, evaluate the sitter. Does he or she seem comfortable with your bird? Does the sitter have experience caring for birds? Does he or she own birds?

Ask for a written contract, and discuss the availability of veterinarian care (does he or she have an existing arrangement with your veterinarian, for example) and what arrangements the sitter makes in the event of inclement weather or personal illness.

Discuss what the sitter's policy is for determining when a pet owner has returned home. Does he or she visit the home until the owners return? Will he or she call to ensure you've arrived home safely and your pets are cared for, or will you have to call and notify the sitter?

If the prospect of leaving your bird with a pet sitter doesn't appeal to you, you may be able to board your bird at your avian veterinarian's office. If boarding services are available, you'll need to determine if you want to risk your bird's health by exposing him to other birds during boarding.

IF YOUR BIRD ESCAPES

One of the most common accidents that befalls bird owners is that a fully flighted bird escapes through an open door or window. Just because your bird has never flown before or shown any interest in leaving his cage doesn't mean that he can't fly or that he won't become disoriented once he's outside.

How can you prevent your bird from becoming lost? First, make sure his wings are safely trimmed at regular intervals. Be sure to trim both wings evenly and remember to trim the wings after your bird has molted. Wing trimming and molting is discussed in chapter 6.

Next, be sure your bird's cage door locks securely and that his cage tray cannot come loose if the cage is knocked over or dropped accidentally. Also be sure that all your window screens fit securely and are free from tears and large holes. Keep all window screens and patio doors closed when your bird is at liberty. Finally, don't ever go outside with your bird on your shoulder.

If, despite your best efforts, your bird should escape, you must act quickly for the best chance of recovering your pet. Here are some steps you can take:

- Have an audiotape of your bird's voice and a portable tape recorder available to lure your bird back home.

- Place your bird's cage in an area where your bird is likely to see it, such as on a deck or patio. Put lots of treats and food on the floor of the cage to tempt your pet back into his home.

- Use another caged bird to attract your parakeet's attention.

- Alert your avian veterinarian's office that your bird has escaped. Also let the local humane society and other veterinary offices in your area know.

- Post fliers in your neighborhood describing your bird. Offer a reward and include your phone number.

- Don't give up hope.

Parakeet Particulars

COMMON PARAKEET BEHAVIORS

The following common parakeet behaviors are listed in alphabetical order to help you better understand your new feathered friend!

Beak Grinding

If you hear your bird making odd little grinding noises as she's drifting off to sleep, don't be alarmed! Beak grinding is a sign of a contented parakeet, and it's commonly heard as a bird settles in for the night.

Beak Wiping

After a meal, it's common for a parakeet to wipe her beak against a perch or on the cage floor to clean it. If something particularly persistent is stuck to a parakeet's beak, she will use her foot to clean her beak.

Eye Pinning

Eye pinning is what happens when your parakeet sees something that excites her. Her pupils will be large, then contract, then go large again. Birds will pin their eyes when they see a favorite food, a favorite person, another bird or a special toy. In larger parrots, this can also be a sign of confused emotions that can leave an owner vulnerable to a nasty bite.

Feather Picking

Don't confuse feather picking with preening (see below). Feather picking results from physiological problems, such as a dietary imbalance, a hormonal change, a thyroid problem or an infection of the skin or feathers. It can also be caused by an emotional upset, such as a change in the owner's appearance, a change in the bird's routine, another pet being added to the home, a new baby in the home or a number of other factors. Once feather picking begins, it may be difficult to get a bird to stop. Although it looks painful to us, some birds find the routine of pulling out their feathers emotionally soothing. The good news is that parakeets are not as prone to this condition as other larger parrots are. If you keep more than one parakeet, however, be aware that they sometimes pick out each other's feathers. If this occurs, you may have to house your birds in separate cages to allow the plucked bird to regrow her plumage.

Fluffing

Fluffing is often a prelude to preening or a tension releaser. If your bird fluffs up, stays fluffed and resembles a little feathered pine cone, however, contact your avian veterinarian for

FEATHERED WARNINGS

Your bird's feathers are one of the most fascinating organs of her body. The bird uses feathers for movement, warmth and balance, among other things. The following are some feather-related behaviors that can indicate health problems for your parakeet.

Fluffing: A healthy parakeet will fluff before preening or for short periods. If your parakeet seems to remain fluffed up for an extended period, see your avian veterinarian. This can be a sign of illness in birds.

Mutual preening: Two birds will preen each other affectionately, but if you notice excessive feather loss, make sure one bird is not picking on the other and pulling out healthy feathers.

Feather picking: A healthy bird will preen often to keep her feathers in top shape. However, a bird under stress may start to preen excessively, and severe feather loss can result.

Mutual preening is a common grooming behavior between cagemates, and sometimes between a bird and her owner.

32

pet. To prevent your parakeet from becoming a problem pet, be sure to provide her the opportunity to entertain herself in her cage alone from time to time. Don't reward her screaming for attention (you'll soon learn which screams are just for the joy of making noise and which ones indicate a pet in danger or pain), and don't bribe your pet into silence with treats while you are out of the room or on the phone. If you do, your bird will soon have you wrapped around her wing feathers and will take full advantage of the situation.

an appointment because fluffed feathers can be an indicator of illness.

Jealousy

Some parakeets become very possessive of their owners, and these jealous birds demonstrate their displeasure in a number of ways. These can include tearing up their cages, nibbling on their owners' hands or screaming that, while not as annoying as the noise made by a cockatoo or macaw, can nonetheless diminish your enjoyment of your parakeet as a

Mutual Preening

This is part of the preening behavior described below, and it can take place between birds or between birds and their owners. It is a sign of affection reserved for best friends or mates, so consider it an honor if your parakeet wants to preen your eyebrows, hair, mustache or beard, or your arms and hands.

Pair Bonding

Not only mated pairs bond, but best bird buddies of the same sex will demonstrate some of the same behavior, including sitting close to each other, preening each other and mimicking the other's actions, such as stretching or scratching, often at the same time.

Preening

Preening is part of a parakeet's normal routine. You will see your bird ruffling and straightening her feathers each day. She will also take oil from the uropygial or preen gland at the base of her tail and spread the oil on the rest of her feathers, so don't be concerned if you see your pet seeming to peck or bite at her tail. If, during molting, your bird seems to remove whole feathers, don't panic! Old, worn feathers are pushed out by incoming new ones, which makes the old feathers loose and easy to remove.

Regurgitating

If you see that your bird is pinning her eyes, bobbing her head and pumping her neck and crop muscles, she is about to regurgitate some food for you. Birds regurgitate to their mates during breeding season and to their young while raising chicks. It is a mark of great affection to have your bird regurgitate her dinner for you, so try not to be too disgusted if your pet starts bringing up her last meal for you.

Resting on One Foot

Do not be alarmed if you see your parakeet occasionally resting on only one foot. This is normal behavior (the resting foot is often drawn up into the belly feathers). If you see your bird always using both feet to perch, please contact your avian veterinarian because this can indicate a health problem.

Side-stepping

Side-stepping is a common movement when a parakeet is working her way across her cage on a perch. Other common movements include climbing and flying (if the cage is large enough).

Scratching

Parakeets have remarkably flexible leg joints, which they sometimes use to bring their legs up and behind their wings to scratch their heads. Parakeets may be the only psittacine

33

birds that do this; larger parrots bring their heads and feet together in front of their bodies to scratch.

Stress

Stress can show itself in many ways in your bird's behavior, including shaking, diarrhea, rapid breathing, wing and tail fanning, screaming, feather picking, poor sleeping habits or loss of appetite. Over a period of time, stress can harm your parakeet's health. To prevent your bird from becoming stressed, try to provide her with as normal and regular a routine as possible. Parrots are, for the most part, creatures of habit, and they don't always adapt well to sudden changes in their environment or schedule. But if you do have to change something, talk to your parrot about it first. It seems crazy, but telling your bird what you're going to do before you do it may actually help reduce her stress.

Stretching

All parrots are prone to sudden bouts of stretching. An otherwise calm bird will suddenly grab the cage bars and stretch the wing and leg muscles on one side of her body, or she will raise both wings high.

Vocalization

Many parrots vocalize around sunrise and sunset, which some believe hearkens back to flock behavior in the wild when wild parrots call to each other to start and end their days. Parakeets are no exceptions to this rule, especially at day's end when they chirp softly as they ready themselves for sleep. If you keep more than one parakeet, you may also notice that the birds will call to each other during the day if they are in separate rooms (perhaps one is on a play gym in the family room while the other is in her cage in the dining room). These contact calls help birds keep track of each other, both in the wild and in your home. If something startles your parakeet, you may hear her make a short, shrill call to signal that something has alarmed her. Parakeets can also express their pleasure or displeasure through vocalization. Soft chirps indicate a happy bird, while shrieks indicate that something is amiss in your bird's world.

TAMING YOUR PARAKEET

Taming a parrot is one of the most popular topics of discussion between avian behaviorists and their clients in bird club meetings, books and magazine articles and on the Internet.

Training a parakeet (or any bird) takes a great deal of time and patience on the part of the bird owner. You must first gain your pet's trust, and then you must work to never lose it. To maintain this, you must be careful not to lose your temper with your bird and never hit her. Birds are very sensitive, intelligent creatures that do not deserve to be hit, no matter how you may feel in a moment of anger.

Although parrots are clever creatures, they are not linear "cause and effect" thinkers. If a parrot commits action A (chewing on some molding under your kitchen cabinets, for example), she won't associate reaction B (you yelling at her, locking her in her cage or otherwise punishing her) with the original misbehavior. As a result, most traditional forms of discipline are ineffective with parrots.

So what do you do when your parakeet misbehaves? Try to catch her in the act. Look at her sternly

Before attempting to train your parakeet, you must first gain your pet's trust through patient and careful interaction.

To remove your parakeet from her cage, begin by first placing your hand in the cage and letting your pet adjust to your "intrusion" for a few moments.

(what bird behaviorist Sally Blanchard calls "the evil eye") and tell her "No" in a firm voice. If the bird is climbing on or chewing something she shouldn't, also remove her from the source of danger and temptation as you tell her "No." If your bird has wound herself up into a screaming banshee, sometimes a little time-out in her cage (between five and ten minutes in most cases) with the cover on does wonders to calm her down. Once the screaming stops and the bird calms down enough to play quietly, eat or simply move around her cage,

the cover comes off to reveal a well-behaved, calmed-down pet.

A good first step in taming your parakeet is getting her to become comfortable around you. To do this, give your bird a bit of warning before you approach her cage. Don't sneak up on your bird, and try not to startle her. Call her name when you walk into the room. Try to be quiet and to move slowly around your pet because these gestures will help her become more comfortable with you. Keep your hands behind you, and reassure the bird that you aren't there to harm her, that everything is all right and that she's a wonderful pet.

After your bird is comfortable having you in the same room with her, you may want to try placing your hand in her cage as a first step toward taking her out of her cage. Place your hand in your bird's cage and hold it there for a few seconds. Don't be surprised if your bird flutters around and squawks at first at the "intruder."

Continue this process daily, and leave your hand in the cage for slightly longer periods of time each day. Within a few days, your parakeet won't make a fuss about your hand being in her space, and she may come over to investigate this new perch. Do not remove your hand from the bird cage the first time your parakeet lands on it; just let the bird become accustomed to perching on your hand.

After several successful perching attempts on successive days, try to take your hand out of the cage with your bird on it. Some parakeets will take to this new adventure willingly, while others are reluctant to leave the safety and security of home. (Be sure your bird's wings are clipped and all doors and windows are secured before taking your bird out of her cage.)

If your bird doesn't seem to respond to this method, you can try an alternate taming method. Take the bird out of her cage and into a small room, such as a bathroom, that has been bird-proofed (i.e., the toilet lid is down, the shower door is closed and the bathroom hasn't been cleaned recently with any strong chemical cleansers). Sit down on the floor, place your bird in front of you and begin playing with the bird. Don't be surprised if your bird tries to fly a few times. With clipped wings, however, she won't get very far and will give up trying after a few failed attempts.

Breeder Charlene Beane advocates a simple and effective taming method. Charlene will hold a bird that isn't quite tame close to her chest so the bird can hear her heartbeat, which seems to calm the bird. She then talks to her in a low, soothing tone and explains to her that she will make someone a wonderful pet. As she does this, she gently begins to stroke the parakeet's back, which helps the bird to relax. She continues to explain her role as a perfect pet for about five minutes, stroking her as she talks. Pretty soon, the bird is calm and ready to be handled.

Once you've calmed your parakeet using Charlene's method, see if you can make perching on your hand a game for your pet. Once she masters perching on your hand, you can teach her to step up by gently pressing your finger up and into the bird's belly. This will cause the bird to step up. As she does so, say "Step up" or "Up." Before long, your bird will respond to this command without much prompting.

Along with the Up command, you may want to teach your parakeet the Down command. When you put the bird down on her cage or play gym, simply say "Down" as the bird steps off your hand. These two simple commands offer a great deal of control for you over your bird, because you can say "Up" to put an unruly bird back in her cage or you can tell a parrot that needs to go to bed "Down" as you put the bird in her cage at night.

After your bird has mastered the Up and Down commands, encourage her to climb a "ladder" by moving her from index finger to index finger (the "rungs"). Keep taming sessions short (about ten minutes is the maximum parakeet

Holding an anxious, or simply an untame, parakeet against your chest so she can hear your heartbeat will help her calm down.

attention span), and make the taming process fun because it will be much more enjoyable for both of you.

After your pet has become comfortable sitting on your hand, try petting her. Birds seem to like to have their heads, backs, cheek patches, under wing areas and eye areas (including the closed eyelids) scratched or petted lightly. Quite a few like to have a spot low on their backs at the base of their tails (over their preen glands) rubbed. Many birds do not enjoy having their stomachs scratched, although yours may think this is heaven! You'll have to experiment to see where your bird likes to be petted. You'll know you're successful if your bird clicks or grinds her beak, pins her eyes or settles onto your hand or into your lap with a completely relaxed, blissful expression on her face.

While some people may try to tell you that you need to wear gloves when taming your parakeet, wearing gloves is probably ill-advised. A parakeet generally doesn't bite that hard, and wearing gloves will only make your hands appear more scary to your bird. If your pet is scared, taming her will take more time and patience on your part, which may make the process less enjoyable for you.

Toilet Training

Although some people don't believe it, parakeets and other parrots can be toilet trained so they don't defecate on their owners. If you want to toilet train your bird, you will have to choose a phrase that will indicate the act of defecating to your pet, such as "Go poop" or "Go potty." While you're training your pet to associate the chosen phrase with the action, you will have to train yourself to your parakeet's body language and actions that indicate she is about to defecate, such as shifting around or squatting slightly.

Once your bird seems to associate "Go potty" with defecating, you can try picking her up and holding her until she starts to shift or squat. Tell the bird to "Go potty" while placing her on her cage, where she can defecate. Once she's done, pick her up again and praise her for being such a smart bird! Expect a few accidents while you are both learning this trick, and soon you'll have a toilet-trained bird that you can put on her cage about every

You can teach your parakeet to perch on your hand by using simple Up and Down commands.

39

twenty minutes or so, give her the command and expect the bird to defecate on command.

WILL MY PARAKEET TALK?

One of the most appealing aspects of parakeet ownership is this species' reputation as talented talkers. Although many parakeets learn to talk, none of them is guaranteed to talk. The tips offered below will help you teach your parakeet to talk, but please don't be disappointed if your pet never utters a word.

Although most parakeets raised around humans do learn to talk, some choose to make other sounds. Some birds choose to imitate the sound of a ringing doorbell, a computer printer or other mechanical noises.

According to parakeet breeder Penny Corbett, the best time to teach a parakeet to talk is between the time she leaves the nest and her first birthday. If you have an adult parakeet, the chances of her learning to talk are not as great as those of a young bird. Male birds may be more likely to talk, but there are some talkative females, too.

Talking Training Tips

You will be more successful in training a parakeet to talk if you keep a single pet bird, rather than a pair. Birds kept in pairs or groups are more likely to bond with other birds than with people. Similarly, don't give your bird any toys with mirrors on them if you want the bird to learn to talk, because your bird will think that the bird in the mirror is a potential cagemate with whom she can bond.

Start with a young bird because the younger the bird is, the more likely she is to want to mimic human speech.

Pick one phrase to start with. Keep it short and simple, such as the bird's name. Say the phrase slowly so the bird learns it clearly. Some people teach their parakeets to talk by rattling off words and phrases quickly, only to be disappointed when the bird repeats them in a blurred jumble that cannot be understood.

Be sure to say the chosen phrase with emphasis and enthusiasm. Birds like a "drama reward" and seem to learn words that are said emphatically, which may be why some of them pick up bad language so quickly!

Try to have phrases make sense. For instance, say "Good morning" or "Hello" when you uncover the bird's cage each day. Say "Good-bye" when you leave the room, or ask "Want a treat?" when you offer your parakeet her meals. (Phrases that make sense are also more likely to be used by you and other members of your family when conversing with your bird. The more often your bird hears an interesting word or phrase, the more likely she is to say that phrase some day.)

Don't change the phrase. If you're teaching your bird to say "Hello," for example, don't say "Hello" one day, then "Hi" the next, followed by "Hi Petey!" (or whatever your bird's name is) another day.

Keep training sessions short. Parakeet breeders recommend ten- to fifteen-minute sessions.

Train your bird in a quiet area. Think of how distracting it is when someone is trying to talk to you with a radio or television blaring in the background. It's hard to hear what the other person is saying under those conditions, isn't it? Your parakeet won't be able to hear you any better or understand what you are trying to accomplish if you try to train her in the midst of noisy distractions. Be sure to keep your parakeet involved in your family's routine, though, because isolating her completely won't help her feel comfortable and part of the family. Remember that a bird needs to feel comfortable in her environment before she will draw attention to herself by talking.

Be patient with your pet. Stop the sessions if you find you are getting frustrated. Your parakeet will sense that something is bothering you and will react by becoming bothered herself. This is not an ideal situation for you or your bird. Try to keep your mood upbeat. Smile a lot and praise your pet when she does well!

Graduate to more difficult phrases as your bird masters simple words. Consider keeping a log of the words your bird knows. (This is especially helpful if more than one person will be working with the parakeet.)

When you aren't talking to your parakeet, try listening to her. Parakeets and other birds sometimes mumble to themselves to practice talking as they drift off to sleep. Because a parakeet has a very small voice, you'll have to listen carefully

DR. IRENE PEPPERBERG AND ALEX

An African Grey named Alex, who is being studied by Irene M. Pepperberg, Ph.D., at the University of Arizona, has a 100-word vocabulary, can count to six and correctly answer questions about the size, shape, color and number of objects shown him. He can categorize objects, telling a questioner what traits the objects have in common or how they differ. Not bad for a "birdbrain"!

to hear if your pet is making progress.

The "talking" tapes and compact discs sold in pet stores and through advertisements in bird magazines sometimes help a bird to learn to talk. Some birds learn from the repetition of the tapes and CDs that, fortunately, have gotten livelier and more interesting in recent years. Other birds benefit from having their owners make tapes of the phrases the bird is currently learning and hearing those tapes play when their owners aren't around. It is not, however, a good idea to play a constant barrage of taped phrases during the day, because the bird is likely to get bored hearing the same thing for hours on end. If she's bored, the bird will be more likely to tune out the tape and the training in the process.

Finally, if your patient, consistent training seems to be going nowhere, you may have to accept the fact that your parakeet isn't going to talk. Your bird may simply not choose to

mimic you even if you do everything right. As one bird lover explained it, "talking should be the icing on the cake," rather than the primary reason for owning a bird. If you end up with a nontalking pet, continue to love her for the unique creature that she is, rather than for what you want her to be.

Talking Success Stories

Although parakeets aren't guaranteed to talk, Puck, a parakeet in northern California, holds the Guinness World Record for largest vocabulary of any animal. Puck's owner estimates that her bird has a 1,728-word vocabulary!

Sparkie, a parakeet that lived in Great Britain from 1954 to 1962, held the record for a talking bird in his time. He won the BBC's Cage Word Contest in 1958 by reciting eight four-line nursery rhymes without stopping. At the time of his death, Sparkie had a vocabulary of 531 words and 383 sentences.

Positively Nutritious

A Healthy Diet

People do not live by bread alone, and birds can't prosper on a diet of seeds and water. Think how dull and unhealthy a one-item diet would be for you—it isn't any more interesting for your parakeet.

Poor diet also causes a number of health problems (respiratory infections, poor feather condition, flaky skin and reproductive problems, to name a few) and is one of the main reasons some parakeets live fairly short lives. If you offer your parakeet a varied diet, you will go a long way to lengthening his life span.

Here's what the Association of Avian Veterinarians recommends as a healthy parakeet diet: 50 percent seed, grain and legumes; 45 percent dark green or dark orange vegetables and fruits; and 5 percent meat (well cooked, please), eggs (also well cooked) or dairy products.

Whatever healthy fresh foods you offer your parakeet, be sure to remove any leftover food from the cage promptly to prevent spoilage and to help keep your bird healthy. Ideally, you should change the food in your bird's cage every two to four hours (about every thirty minutes in warm weather), so a parakeet should be all right with a tray of food to pick through in the morning, another to select from during the afternoon and a fresh salad to nibble on for dinner.

Seeds and Grains

The seeds, grain and legumes portion of your parakeet's diet can include clean, fresh seed from your local pet supply store. Give your pet his seeds in a clean, dry dish, and check the dish daily to ensure your parakeet has enough food. Don't just look in the dish, but actually remove it from the cage and blow lightly into the dish (you might want to do this over the kitchen sink or the trash can) to remove seed hulls. Parakeets are notorious for giving the impression that they have enough food. Because they are such neat eaters and drop the used hulls right back in their dishes, they can often fool you.

One foodstuff that is very popular with parakeets is millet, especially millet sprays. These golden sprays are part treat and part toy. Offer your parakeet this treat sparingly, however, because it is high in fat and can make your parakeet pudgy! Other items in the bread group that you can offer your pet include unsweetened breakfast cereals, whole-wheat bread, cooked beans, cooked rice and pasta.

Fruits and Vegetables

Dark green or dark orange vegetables and fruits contain vitamin A, which is an important part of a bird's diet and is missing from the seeds, grains and legumes group. This vitamin helps fight off infection and keeps a bird's eyes, mouth

Refill your parakeet's food dish with fresh seeds daily.

44

and respiratory system healthy. Some vitamin A–rich foods are carrots, yams, sweet potatoes, broccoli, dried red peppers, dandelion greens and spinach.

Some birds will eat frozen vegetables and fruits, while others turn their beaks up at the somewhat mushy texture of these foodstuffs. The high sodium content in some canned foods may make them unhealthy for your parakeet. Frozen and canned foods will serve your bird's needs in an emergency, but you should offer only fresh foods on a regular basis.

Protein

Along with small portions of the well-cooked meat, you can also offer your parakeet bits of tofu, water-packed tuna, fully scrambled eggs, cottage cheese, unsweetened yogurt or low-fat cheese. Don't overdo the dairy products, though, because a bird's digestive system lacks the enzyme lactase, which means he is unable to fully process dairy foods.

FOOD TABOOS

As is evident, there is a wide variety of foods that are good for your bird.

SPROUTING

You can test the seed for freshness by sprouting some of them in some water on your windowsill. Soak the seeds thoroughly with water and drain the excess. In two or three days, fresh seeds will sprout; stale seeds won't. After the fresh seeds sprout, you can rinse them well and feed them to your parakeets, too. Immediately discard any sprouts that smell unappetizing or grow mold; these are unhealthy to feed to your parakeet.

45

There are, however, some foods that aren't healthy for your parakeet, and these should be avoided. Do not feed alcohol, rhubarb or avocado (the skin and the area around the pit can be toxic) to your pet. Don't give your parakeet any foods that are highly salted, sweetened or fatty (such as pretzels, candy or potato chips). Do *not* give your bird chocolate. Chocolate contains a chemical, theobromine, that birds cannot digest as completely as people can. In fact, chocolate can kill your parakeet, so resist the temptation to share this snack with your pet. You will also want to avoid giving your bird seeds or pits from apples, apricots, cherries, peaches, pears and

Millet sprays are nice treats, but are higher in fat, so offer this treat sparingly.

Sharing healthy people food with your parakeet is completely acceptable, but do not share food that you have bitten. Human saliva contains bacteria that are perfectly normal for people but are potentially toxic to birds, so please don't give partially eaten food to your pet. For your bird's health and your peace of mind, offer him a separate portion.

ENTICING THE OLDER PARAKEET

If you've adopted an older parakeet that eats primarily seeds, try offering your bird some of the fruits and vegetables that are popular with many parrots, such as apple slices, grapes or corn. You can offer a small slice of apple that you've dipped in seeds, a halved grape or some fresh corn kernels. Although these fruits and vegetables are not as rich in important vitamins as their dark green or dark orange counterparts, they can help bridge the gap between seeds and a more varied diet for fussy eaters. To ease the stress of relocating to your home, try to feed your parakeet a diet as close to the one he ate in his previous home. To help your bird adjust even faster, you may

plums, because they contain toxins that can be harmful to your pet's health.

SHARING PEOPLE FOOD

Let common sense be your guide in choosing which foods can be offered to your bird: If it's healthy for you, it's probably permissible to share. However, remember to reduce the size of the portion you offer to your bird—a few shreds of grated carrot or squash, a piece or two of cereal, or a few cooked beans will be more appealing to your parakeet than a larger, human-sized portion.

want to sprinkle some food on the cage floor, because parakeets sometimes revert to their natural ground-feeding habits in times of stress.

THE PELLETED DIET OPTION

You're probably asking, "Just what is a pellet, anyway?" Don't birds just eat seeds? While seeds are an important part of many birds' diets, some parakeet owners prefer to feed their pets a pelleted diet rather than a mixture of seeds, vegetables, fruits and healthful table food.

Pelleted diets are created by mixing a variety of healthful ingredients into a mash and then forcing (or extruding) the hot mixture through a machine to form various shapes. Some pelleted diets have colors and flavors added, while others are fairly plain. These formulated diets provide more balanced nutrition for your pet bird in an easy-to-serve form that reduces the amount of wasted food and eliminates the chance for a bird to pick through a smorgasbord of healthful foods to find his favorites and reject the less appealing foods. Some parakeets accept pelleted diets quickly,

YOUR PARAKEET'S BEAK

Because parakeets eat primarily seeds and other plant materials (in the wild some parakeets have been seen eating the seeds of twenty-one different species of grasses), their beaks have developed into efficient little seed crackers. Look at the underside of your bird's upper beak. It has tiny ridges in it that help the bird hold and crack seeds easily.

although others require some persuading.

If you want to convert your pet to a pelleted diet, you will want to offer him pellets alongside or mixed with his current diet. (Make sure the parakeet recognizes that pellets are food before proceeding.) Once you see that your bird is eating the pellets, begin to gradually increase the amount of pellets you offer at mealtime while decreasing the amount of other food you serve. Within a few weeks, your bird should be eating his pellets with gusto!

If your parakeet seems a bit finicky about trying pellets, you may have to make him believe that you enjoy pellets as a snack. Really play up your apparent enjoyment of this

47

new food because it will pique your parakeet's curiosity and make the pellets exceedingly interesting to your pet.

If you have another bird in the house that already eats a pelleted diet, place your parakeet's cage where he can watch the other bird enjoy the pellets. Before long, your parakeet will be playing "follow the leader" right to the food bowl. Finally, you may want to roll a favorite treat, such as a damp broccoli floret or an apple slice, in pellets and offer this decorated piece of produce to your pet.

Whatever you do, don't starve your bird into trying a new food. Offer a variety of new foods consistently, along with familiar favorites. This will ensure that your bird is eating and will also encourage him to try new foods. Don't be discouraged if your parakeet doesn't dive right into a new food. Be patient, keep offering new foods to your bird and praise him enthusiastically when he is brave enough to sample something new!

GRIT

As a new bird owner, you may hear a lot of talk about the importance of grit in your bird's diet. Birds use grit in their gizzards to grind their food, much as we use our teeth. How much grit birds need and how often it should be offered to them is a source of contention among avian veterinarians and bird breeders. Some will tell you birds need grit regularly, while others will advise against it. If your parakeet's breeder and your avian veterinarian think your bird requires grit, offer it sparingly (only about a pinch every

Fruits and vegetables rich in vitamin A are an essential part of your parakeet's diet.

Your parakeet needs fresh water to drink each day.

few weeks). Do not offer it daily, and do not provide your parakeet with a separate dish of grit because some birds will overeat the grit and suffer dangerous crop impactions as a result.

SUPPLEMENTS

You may also be concerned about whether your bird is receiving adequate amounts of vitamins and minerals in his diet. This is of particular concern if your parakeet is eating a seed-based diet. Parakeets on pelleted or formulated diets should have all their vitamin and mineral needs met with these special diets, so additional supplements are unnecessary. If your parakeet's diet is mainly seeds, however, you may want to sprinkle a good-quality vitamin-and-mineral powder onto your pet's fresh foods, where it is likely to adhere and therefore more likely to be eaten. Vitamin-enriched seed diets may provide some supplementation, but some of them add the vitamins and minerals to the seed hull, which your pet will remove and discard while he's eating. Before supplementing your bird's diet with vitamins and minerals, consult with your pet's veterinarian.

Pretty Birdie

Your parakeet has several grooming needs. She must be able to bathe regularly, and she will need to have her nails and flight feathers trimmed periodically to ensure her safety.

Although some people would say that a parakeet's beak also needs trimming, a healthy bird that has enough chew toys should do a good job of keeping her beak trimmed on her own. If your parakeet's beak becomes overgrown, though, please consult your avian veterinarian. A parrot's beak contains a surprising number of blood vessels, so beak trimming is best left to the experts. Also, a suddenly overgrown beak may indicate that your bird is suffering from liver damage, a virus or scaly mites, all of which require veterinary care.

PREENING

Preening is one of your parakeet's ways of keeping herself well-groomed. You will notice her ruffling and straightening her feathers each day. She will also take oil from the gland at the base of her tail and spread it on the rest of her feathers, so don't be concerned if you see your parakeet apparently pecking or biting at her tail. Preening, combined with your assistance in bathing, nail clipping and wing clipping will keep your parakeet in top shape.

BATHING YOUR PARAKEET

You can bathe your parakeet in a variety of ways. You can mist her lightly with a clean spray bottle filled with warm water only, or you can allow her to bathe in the kitchen or bathroom sink under a slow stream of water. Many parakeets prefer to bathe in their cages, either in a small flat saucer of warm water, a plastic parakeet bathtub or an enclosed bird bath that you can purchase in your local pet store. Bathing is important to birds to help them keep their feathers clean and healthy, so don't deny your pet the chance to bathe!

Unless your parakeet has gotten herself into oil, paint, wax or some other substance that elbow grease alone won't remove and that could harm her feathers, she will not require soap as part of her bath.

Let your bird bathe early in the day so she has an opportunity to let her feathers dry completely before the evening comes. In cooler weather, you may want help the process along by drying your parakeet off with a blow dryer—set the blow dryer on low and keep it moving. Your parakeet may soon learn that drying off is the most enjoyable part of her bath!

NAIL TRIMMING

Trimming your parakeet's nails is a fairly simple procedure. Parakeets and other parrots need their nails clipped occasionally to prevent the nails from catching on toys or

51

Your parakeet will enjoy an occasional bath in a sink filled with a little warm water.

If you're not sure how to trim your bird's nails, have your veterinarian show you.

possible. Stop well before you reach the quick. If you do happen to cut the nail short enough to make it bleed, apply cornstarch or flour, followed by direct pressure, to stop the bleeding.

WING TRIMMING

The goal of a properly done wing trim is to prevent your pet from flying away or flying into a window, mirror or wall while she's out of her cage. An added benefit of trimming your pet's wings is that her inability to fly well will make her more dependent on you for transportation, which should make her easier to handle. However, the bird still needs enough wing feathers so that she can glide safely to the ground if she is startled and takes flight from her cage top or play gym.

Because this is a delicate procedure, it is best to enlist the help of your avian veterinarian, at least the first time your bird gets a wing trim.

The first step in wing feather trimming is to assemble all the things you will need and to find a quiet, well-lit place to groom your pet before you catch and trim her. Having good light to work under will make your job easier, and

perches and injuring themselves. Unlike some of the larger parrots, parakeet nails are light in color, which makes it easier for owners to see where the nail stops and the blood and blood supply (or quick) begins. In parakeets, the quick is generally seen as a pink color inside the nail.

You will need to only remove tiny portions of the nail to keep your parakeet's claws trimmed. Generally, a good guideline to follow is to only remove the hook on each nail, and to do this in the smallest increments having a quiet work area may help calm down your parakeet and make her a bit easier to handle. Your grooming tools will include:

- a washcloth or small towel to wrap your parakeet in

- small, sharp scissors to do the actual trimming

- needle-nosed pliers (to pull any blood feathers you may cut accidentally)

- flour or cornstarch to act as a styptic powder in case a blood feather is cut

- nail trimmers (while you have your bird in the towel, you might as well do her nails, too)

Once you've assembled your supplies, drape the towel over your hand and catch your parakeet with your toweled hand. Grab your bird by the back of her head and neck, and wrap her in the towel. Hold the bird's head securely with your thumb and index finger. (Having the bird's head covered by a towel will calm her and will give her something to chew on while you clip her wings.)

Lay the bird on her back, being careful not to constrict or compress her chest (remember, birds have no

GROOMING TIPS

- Groom your pet in a quiet, well-lit place.

- Have all the necessary grooming supplies on hand before you begin.

- Make sure you have styptic powder on hand.

- Check wings and toenails regularly to see if they need retrimming.

diaphragms to help them breathe), and spread her wing out carefully to look for new feathers that are still growing in, also called blood feathers. These can be identified by their waxy, tight look (new feathers in their feather sheaths resemble the end of a shoelace) and their dark centers or quills, which are caused by the blood supply to the new feather.

If your bird has a number of blood feathers, you may want to put off trimming her wings for a few days, because older, fully grown feathers act as a cushion to protect those just coming in from life's hard knocks. If your bird has only one or two blood feathers, you can trim the full-grown feathers accordingly. *Never trim a blood feather.*

53

To trim your bird's feathers, separate each one away from the other flight feathers and cut it individually (remember, the goal is to have a well-trimmed bird that's still able to glide a bit if she needs to). Use the primary coverts (the set of feathers above the primary flight feathers on your bird's wing) as a guideline as to how short you should trim.

Cut the first five to eight flight feathers starting from the tip of the wing, and be sure to trim an equal number of feathers from each wing. Although some people think that a bird needs only one trimmed wing, this is incorrect and potentially dangerous.

If you do happen to cut a blood feather, remain calm. You must remove it and stop the bleeding to ensure that your bird doesn't bleed to death, and panicking will do neither of you much good.

To remove a blood feather, take a pair of needle-nosed pliers and grasp the broken feather's shaft as close to the skin of the bird's wing as you can. With one steady motion, pull the feather out completely. After you've removed the feather, put a pinch of flour or cornstarch on the feather follicle (the spot you pulled the feather out of) and apply direct pressure for a few minutes until the bleeding stops. If the bleeding

Wing trimming is a delicate procedure, and as such should be performed by you only if you've been shown how to do it by your avian veterinarian.

doesn't stop after doing so, or if you can't remove the feather shaft, contact your avian veterinarian for further instructions.

Although it may seem like you're hurting your parakeet by removing the broken blood feather, consider this: A broken blood feather is like an open faucet. If left in, the faucet stays open and lets the blood out. Once removed, the bird's skin generally closes up behind the feather shaft and shuts off the faucet.

Now that you've trimmed your bird's wing feathers, congratulate yourself. You've just taken a great step toward keeping your bird safe. But don't rest on your laurels just yet; you must remember to check your parakeet's wing feathers and retrim them periodically (at least four times a year).

MOLTING

At least once a year, your parakeet will lose her feathers. Don't be alarmed, because this is a normal process called molting. Many pet birds seem to be in an almost perpetual molt, with feathers falling out and coming in throughout the summer.

You can consider your bird in molting season when you see a lot of whole feathers in the bottom of the cage and you notice that your bird seems to have broken out in a rash of stubbly little aglets (resembling the plastic tips on the ends of your shoelaces). These are the feather sheaths that help new pinfeathers break through the skin, and they are made of keratin (the same material that makes up our fingernails). The sheaths help protect growing feathers from damage until the feather completes its growth cycle.

You may notice that your parakeet is a little more irritable during the molt; this is to be expected. Think about how you would feel if you had all these itchy new feathers coming in all of a sudden.

Be particularly alert for the need to trim your bird's wings after a molt, because she will have a whole new crop of flight feathers. You'll be able to tell when your parakeet is due for a trim when she starts becoming bolder in her flying attempts.

To Good Health

AVIAN ANATOMY

If you think your body doesn't have much in common with your pet parakeet's, think again. You both have skin; skeletons; respiratory, cardiovascular, digestive, excretory and nervous systems and sensory organs, although the various systems function in slightly different ways.

Skin

Your parakeet's skin is probably pretty difficult to see because your pet has so many feathers. If you part the feathers carefully, though, you can see your pet's thin, transparent skin and the muscles beneath it. Modified skin cells help make up your bird's beak, cere, claws and the scales on his feet and legs.

Skeletal System

Next, let's look at your bird's skeleton. Did you know that some bird bones are hollow? This makes them lighter and makes flying easier, but it also means that these bones can be more susceptible to breakage. For this reason, you must always handle your bird carefully! Another adaptation for flight is that the bones of a bird's wing (which correspond to our arm and hand bones) are fused for greater strength.

Birds have air sacs in some of their bones (these are called pneumatic bones) that help lighten their bodies for flight. They also have air sacs throughout their bodies to cool them efficiently. Birds cannot perspire as mammals do because birds have no sweat glands, so they must have a way to cool off.

Parrots have ten neck vertebrae in contrast to a human's seven. This makes a parrot's neck more free moving than a person's (a parrot can turn his head almost 180 degrees), which can be advantageous to spotting food or predators in the wild.

Respiratory System

Your bird's respiratory system is a highly efficient system that works in a markedly different way from yours. Here's how your parakeet breathes: Air enters the system through your bird's nares, passes through his sinuses and into his throat. As it does, the air is filtered through the choana, which is a slit that can be easily seen in the roof of many birds' mouths. The choana also helps to clean and warm the air before it goes further into the respiratory system.

After the air passes the choana, it flows through the larynx and trachea, past the syrinx or "voice box."

Your bird doesn't have vocal cords like you do; rather, vibration of the syrinx membrane is what allows your bird to make sounds.

As the air continues its journey past the syrinx and into the bronchi, your bird's lungs don't expand and contract to bring the air in. This is partly due to the fact that birds don't have diaphragms like people do. Instead, the bird's body wall expands and contracts, much like a fireplace bellows. This action brings air into the air sacs mentioned earlier. This bellows action also moves air in and out of the lungs.

Although a bird's respiratory system is extremely efficient at exchanging gases in the system, two complete breaths are required to do the same work that a single breath does in people and other mammals.

Cardiovascular System

Along with the respiratory system, your bird's cardiovascular system keeps oxygen and other nutrients moving throughout his body, although the circulatory path in your parakeet differs from yours.

Like you, though, your parakeet has a four-chambered heart, with two atria and two ventricles. Unlike the average human heart rate of seventy-two beats per minute, your parakeet's average heart rate is 350 to 550 beats per minute. According to Dr. Gary Gallerstein, cardiac output (the amount of blood pumped through the heart in a minute) in a flying parakeet is seven times greater than in a human exercising at maximum capacity! Having such efficient respiratory and circulatory systems allows parakeets and other parrots to use incredible amounts of energy very efficiently.

58

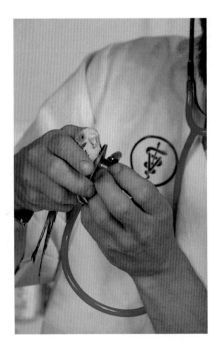

The average heart rate for a parakeet is between 350 and 500 beats per minute.

Digestive System

To keep this energy-efficient machine (your bird's body) running requires fuel (food). This is where your bird's digestive system comes in. One of the main functions of the digestive system is to provide the fuel that maintains your bird's body temperature.

Your parakeet's digestive system begins with his beak. The size and shape of a bird's beak depend on his food-gathering needs. Compare the sharp, pointed beak of an eagle or the elongated bill of a hummingbird with the small, hooked beak of your parakeet.

After the food leaves your bird's mouth, it travels down the esophagus, where it is moistened. The food then travels to the crop, where it is moistened further and is supplied in small increments to the bird's stomach.

After the food leaves the crop, it travels through the proventriculus, where digestive juices are added, to the gizzard, where the food is broken down into even smaller pieces. The food then travels to the small intestine, where nutrients are absorbed into the bloodstream. Anything that's leftover then travels through the large intestine to the cloaca, which is the common chamber that collects wastes before they leave the bird's body through the vent. The whole process from mouth to vent usually takes only a few hours, which is why you may notice that your bird leaves frequent, small droppings in his cage.

Nervous System

Your parakeet's nervous system is very similar to your own. Both consist of the brain, the spinal cord and countless nerves throughout the body that transmit messages to and from the brain.

Feathers

Birds are the only animals that have feathers, which serve several purposes. Feathers help birds fly, they keep birds warm, they attract the attention of potential mates and they help scare away predators.

A feather is a remarkably designed creation. The base of the feather shaft, which fits into the bird's skin, is called the quill. It is light and hollow, but remarkably tough. The upper part of the feather shaft is called the rachis. From it

A parakeet has between 2,000 and 3,000 feathers on his small body.

branch the barbs and barbules (smaller barbs) that make up most of the feather. The barbs and barbules have small hooks on them that enable the different parts of the feather to interlock like Velcro and form the feather's vane or web.

Birds have several different types of feathers on their bodies. Contour feathers are the colorful outer feathers on a bird's body and wings. Many birds have an undercoating of down feathers that helps keep them warm. Semiplume feathers are found on a bird's beak, nares (nostrils) and eyelids.

A bird's flight feathers can be classified into one of two types. Primary flight feathers are the large wing feathers that push a bird forward during flight. They are also the feathers that need clipping (see Chapter 6, "Pretty Birdie," for more information on clipping wings). Secondary flight feathers are found on the inner wing, and they help support the bird in flight. Primary and secondary wing feathers can operate independently of each other. The bird's tail feathers also assist in flight by acting as a brake and a rudder to make steering easier.

Sometimes pet birds will develop white lines or small holes on the large feathers of their wings and tails. These lines or holes are referred to as "stress bars" or "stress lines" and result from the bird experiencing stress as the feathers were developing. If you notice stress bars on your parakeet's feathers, discuss them with your avian veterinarian.

Parakeet Senses

SIGHT

Although a bird has a poor sense of taste, he has a well-developed sense of sight. Birds can see detail and they can discern colors. Be aware of this when selecting cage accessories for your pet, because some parakeets react to a change in the color of their food dishes. Some seem excited by a different color bowl, while others act fearful of the new item.

Because their eyes are located on the sides of their heads, most pet birds rely on monocular vision, which means that they use each eye independently of the other. If a bird really wants to study an object, you will often see him tilt his head to one side and examine the object with just one eye. Birds aren't really able to move their eyes around very much, but they compensate for this by having highly mobile necks that allow them to turn their heads about 180 degrees.

HEARING

You may be wondering where your parakeet's ears are. Look carefully under the feathers behind and below each eye to find them. The ears are the somewhat large holes in the sides of your parakeet's head. Parakeets have about the same ability to distinguish sound waves and determine the location of the sound as people do, but birds seem to be less sensitive to higher and lower pitches than their owners.

SMELL AND TASTE

Birds seem to have poorly developed senses of smell and taste because smells often dissipate quickly in the air (where flying birds spend their time) and because birds have fewer taste buds in their mouths than people do. (Parrot taste buds are located in the roof of the birds' mouths, not in the tongue like ours are.)

TOUCH

The final sense we relate to, touch, is well developed in parrots. Parrots use their feet and their mouths to touch their surroundings (young birds particularly seem to "mouth" everything they can get their beaks on), to play and to determine what is safe to perch on or chew on and what's good to eat.

Along with their tactile uses, a parrot's feet also have an unusual design compared to other caged birds. Do you notice that, unlike a finch or canary, two of your parakeet's toes point forward and two point backward? This two toes forward and two toes back arrangement is called zygodactyl, and it allows a parrot to climb up and down and around in trees easily. Some larger parrots also use their feet to hold food or to play with toys.

VISITING THE VETERINARIAN

With good care, a parakeet can live up to eighteen years, although the average life span of these small par-

Two toes point forward and two toes point backward on a parakeet's foot.

rots is about one-third of that, or six years. One of the reasons parakeets don't live longer is that their owners may be reluctant to take their pets to the veterinarian. Some people don't want to pay veterinary bills on such "inexpensive" birds.

Choosing a Veterinarian

As a caring owner, you want your bird to have good care and the best chance at living a long, healthy life. To that end, you will need to locate a veterinarian who understands the special medical needs of birds and one with whom you can establish a good working relationship. The best time to do this is when you first bring your parakeet home from the breeder or pet store.

If you don't know an avian veterinarian in your area, ask the person from whom you bought your

61

It's wise for your veterinarian to first examine your parakeet while he's still in his cage.

parakeet where he or she takes his or her birds. (Breeders and bird stores usually have avian veterinarians on whom they depend.) Talk to other bird owners you know and find out who they take their pets to, or call bird clubs in your area for referrals.

If you have no bird-owning friends or can't locate a bird club, your next best bet is the Yellow Pages. Read the advertisements for veterinarians carefully, and try to find one who specializes in birds.

Once you've received your recommendations or have found likely

candidates in the telephone book, start calling the veterinary offices. Ask the receptionist how many birds the doctor sees in a week or month, how much an office visit costs, and what payment options are available (cash, credit card, check or time payments). You can also inquire if the doctor keeps birds as his or her personal pets.

If you like the answers you receive from the receptionist, make an appointment for your parakeet to be evaluated. Make a list of any questions you want to ask the doctor regarding diet, how often your bird's wings and nails should be clipped or how often you should bring the bird in for an examination.

Prepare for Your Veterinary Visit

Bird owners should not be afraid to ask their avian veterinarians questions. Avian vets have devoted a lot of time, energy and effort to studying birds, so put this resource to use whenever you can.

What bird owners may not know is that they may be asked a number of questions by the veterinarian. When you take your bird in for an exam, be aware that the doctor may ask you for answers to these questions:

- Why is the bird here today?

- What's the bird's normal activity level like?

- How is the bird's appetite?

- What does the bird usually eat?

- Have you noticed a change in the bird's appearance lately?

Be sure to explain any changes in as much detail as you can, because changes in your bird's normal behavior can indicate illness.

During the initial examination, the veterinarian will probably take his or her first look at your parakeet while he is still in his cage or carrier. The doctor may talk to you and your bird for a few minutes to give the bird an opportunity to become accustomed to him or her, rather than simply reaching right in and grabbing your pet. While the veterinarian is talking to you, he or she will check the bird's posture and his ability to perch.

Next, the doctor should remove the bird from his carrier or cage and look him over carefully. He or she will particularly note the condition of your pet's eyes, his beak and his

nares (nostrils). The bird should be weighed, and the veterinarian will probably palpate (feel) your parakeet's body and wings for any lumps, bumps or deformities that require further investigation. Feather condition will also be assessed, as will the condition of the bird's vent, legs and feet.

Once the examination is concluded and you've had a chance to discuss any questions you have with your veterinarian, the doctor will probably recommend a follow-up examination schedule for your pet. Most healthy birds visit the veterinarian annually.

MEDICATING YOUR PARAKEET

Most bird owners are faced with the prospect of medicating their pets at some point in the birds' lives, and many are unsure if they can complete the task without hurting their pets. If you have to medicate your pet, your avian veterinarian or veterinary technician should explain the process to you. In the course of the explanation, you should find out how you will be administering the medication, the amount of the drug you will be giving your bird, how

63

often the bird needs the medication and how long the entire course of treatment will last.

Oral Medication

Oral medication is a good route to take with birds that are small, easy to handle or underweight. The medication is usually given with a needleless plastic syringe placed in the left side of the bird's mouth and pointed toward the right side of his throat. This route is recommended to ensure that the medication gets into the bird's digestive system and not into his lungs, where aspiration pneumonia can result.

Medicating a bird's food or offering medicated feed (such as tetracyline-laced pellets that were fed to imported birds during quarantine to prevent psittacosis) is another effective possibility, but medications added to a bird's water supply are often less effective because sick birds are less likely to drink water, and the medicated water may have an unusual taste that makes a bird less likely to drink it.

Injected Medication

Avian veterinarians consider injections to be the most effective method of medicating birds. Some injection sites—into a vein, beneath the skin or into a bone—are used by avian veterinarians in the clinic setting. Bird owners are usually asked to medicate their birds intramuscularly, or by injecting medication into the bird's chest muscle. This is the area of the bird's body that has the greatest muscle mass, so it is a good injection site.

Wrap your bird securely, but comfortably, in a washcloth or small towel, and lay him on your lap with

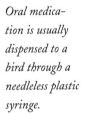

Oral medication is usually dispensed to a bird through a needleless plastic syringe.

his chest up. Hold his head securely with your thumb and index finger of one hand, and use the other to insert the syringe at about a 45 degree angle under the bird's chest feathers and into the muscle beneath.

You should remember to alternate the side you inject your bird on (for example, left in the morning and right in the evening) to ensure that one side doesn't get overinjected and sore, and you should remain calm and talk to your bird in a soothing tone while you're administering the drug.

Topical Medication

Topical medication provides direct, external medication to part of a bird's body. Uses can include medications for eye infections, dry skin on the feet or legs or sinus problems.

PARAKEET HEALTH CONCERNS

Although parakeets are generally hardy birds, they are prone to a few health problems, including scaly face, goiter, gout, obesity and lipomas. They, like all birds, can also suffer from respiratory problems and other conditions that result from a vitamin A deficiency, especially if they consume diets that are high in seeds and low in vitamin A–rich foods. A vitamin A deficiency can be prevented by feeding a varied, healthy diet.

Scaly Face

Scaly face is a condition caused by the *Knemidokoptes* mite, a tiny relative of the spider that likes to burrow into the top layers of a parakeet's skin around his cere, eyelids, vent or legs. This burrowing leaves white crusts on the bird's cere or the corners of the mouth. If allowed to progress, scaly face can cause lesions on a bird's beak, eyelids, throat, vent, legs and feet. Advanced cases can also cause beak deformation and horny appendages on a bird's face and legs. The leg appendages can interfere with a bird's ability to move his legs and toes.

If your avian veterinarian suspects your parakeet has scaly face, he or she will diagnose the condition by examining skin scrapings under a microscope. Although scaly face has the potential to be a serious condition, the good news is that it can be easily treated by a veterinarian using

SIGNS OF ILLNESS

To help your veterinarian and to keep your pet from suffering long-term health risks, keep a close eye on his daily activities and appearance. If something suddenly changes in the way your bird looks or acts, contact your veterinarian immediately. Birds naturally hide signs of illness to protect themselves from predators, so by the time a bird looks or acts sick, he may already be dangerously ill.

Some signs of illness include:

- a fluffed-up appearance
- a loss of appetite
- sleeping all the time
- a change in the appearance or number of droppings
- weight loss
- listlessness
- drooping wings
- lameness
- the bird has partially eaten food stuck to his face or food has been regurgitated onto the cage floor
- labored breathing, with or without tail bobbing
- runny eyes or nose
- the bird stops talking or singing

If your bird shows any of these signs, please contact your veterinarian's office immediately.

Ivermectin, which will remove the mites and restore the skin to its normal appearance.

Goiter

Goiter is an enlargement of the thyroid gland in a bird's throat. It is caused by an iodine deficiency and is most often seen in parakeets that eat seed-only diets. Symptoms include difficulty in breathing, swallowing and regurgitation. Your veterinarian can determine if your parakeet has a goiter through x-rays and blood tests. Iodine supplements are used to treat the condition.

Gout

Gout is associated with kidney malfunction. Specifically, gouty birds have kidneys that are unable to remove excess nitrogen from the bird's bloodstream. This causes uric acid and urates to build up in the bird's body or in his joints. The exact cause of gout is unclear at this time, but high levels of dietary sodium or calcium and inadequate fluid intake may contribute to gout.

Two forms of gout occur: articular gout, which affects a bird's lower leg joints as shiny, cream-colored swellings, and visceral gout, which affects a bird's internal organs and is difficult to diagnose. Articular gout, the type most often seen in parakeets, is a painful condition that causes an affected bird to go lame.

Presently, no cure exists for gout. Treatment includes lowering protein levels and increasing the amount of fruits and vegetables in the bird's diet, along with treating any underlying infections that may have an impact on kidney function. Veterinarians may be able to lower a bird's uric acid levels with medication, and they can also prescribe drugs to ease the bird's pain. Padded perches also seem to offer comfort to afflicted birds.

Obesity

Obesity can sometimes be caused by a malfunctioning thyroid gland, but it is most often caused by a bird eating far more calories than he burns in a day. (English parakeets seem to be more prone to obesity than their American cousins.) To prevent this from happening to your pet parakeet, make sure that he eats a well-balanced diet that is low in oil seeds and nuts (sunflower seeds, millet, peanuts, walnuts) and that he

receives ample opportunity to exercise both inside his cage and outside of it during supervised "out times" on a play gym.

Bumblefoot

Bumblefoot is an infection of the sole of the bird's foot. It can cause redness and inflammation, swelling and lameness. Antibiotics, bandages and surgery may be needed to treat the condition, which can be prevented by keeping a bird's cage clean and feeding him a well-balanced diet.

Giardia

This illness is caused by a protozoan called *Giardia psittaci*. This organism may cause a bird to have loose droppings, lose weight, pick his feathers, lose his appetite and become depressed. Diagnosing this disease can be challenging, because the *Giardia* organism is difficult to detect in a bird's feces. The disease can be spread through contaminated food or water, and birds do not develop an immunity to it. Your veterinarian can recommend an appropriate medication to treat *Giardia*.

French Moult

French moult causes flight and tail feathers to develop improperly or not develop at all. Researchers believe the disease is caused by polyoma virus, which can be spread through contact with new birds, as well as from feather and fecal dust.

Adult birds can carry polyoma virus but not show any signs of the disease. These seemingly healthy birds can pass the virus to young birds that have never been exposed, and these young birds can die from polyoma virus rather quickly. Sick birds can become weak, lose their appetites, bleed beneath the skin, have enlarged abdomens, become paralyzed, regurgitate and have diarrhea. Some birds with polyoma virus die suddenly.

At present, there is no cure, although a vaccine is under development. Protecting your pets against polyoma virus and other diseases is why it's important to quarantine new stock and to take precautions, including showering and changing clothes, before handling your pet when you've been in the presence of other birds.

Papilloma

Papillomas are benign tumors that can appear almost anywhere on a bird's skin, including his foot, leg, eyelid or preen gland. If a bird has a papilloma on his cloaca, the bird may appear to have a "wet raspberry" coming out of his vent. These tumors, which are caused by a virus, can appear as small, crusty lesions, or they may be raised growths that have a bumpy texture or small projections.

Many papillomas can be left untreated without harm to the bird, but some must be removed by an avian veterinarian because a bird may pick at the growth and cause it to bleed.

Psittacine Beak and Feather Disease Syndrome (PBFDS)

This virus was first detected in cockatoos and was originally thought to be a cockatoo-specific problem. It has since been determined that more than forty species of parrots, including parakeets, can contract this disease, which causes a bird's feathers to become pinched or clubbed in appearance. Other symptoms include beak fractures and mouth ulcers. This highly contagious, fatal disease is most common in birds less than 3 years of age, and there is no cure at present.

HOUSEHOLD HAZARDS

One of the reasons you chose your parakeet as a pet is because he is such a curious, active little bird. This curiosity and activity can lead your pet into all sorts of mischief around your home, some of which can be harmful to your bird.

This doesn't mean you shouldn't let your pet out of his cage. On the contrary, all parrots need time out of their cages to maintain physical and mental health. The key to keeping your pet safe and healthy is to watch over him and play with him when he's out of his cage. Both of you will come to enjoy these playtimes greatly.

Some household hazards to be aware of (dangers to parakeets are included in parentheses) include:

- unscreened windows and doors (escape potential)

- mirrors (collision and injury potential)

- exposed electrical cords (possible electrocution if chewed on)

- toxic houseplants (poisoning)

AVOID MITE PROTECTORS

Mite protectors that hang on a bird's cage or conditioning products applied directly to a bird's feathers are not really necessary to keep your parakeet healthy. Well-cared-for birds don't have mites and shouldn't be in danger of contracting them. (If your parakeet does have mites, veterinary care is the most effective method of treatment.) Moreover, the fumes from some of these products are quite strong and can be harmful to your pet's health. Conditioners, anti-picking products and other substances that are applied to your bird's feathers will serve one purpose: to get your bird to preen himself so thoroughly in an effort to remove the offending liquid from his feathers that he could remove all his feathers in a particular area. If you want to encourage your bird to preen regularly and help condition his feathers, simply mist the bird regularly with clean, warm water or hold him under a gentle stream from a faucet. Your parakeet will take care of the rest.

- unattended ashtrays (burns from lit cigarettes or poisoning from ingested cigarette butts)

- venetian blind cords (hanging)

- sliding glass doors (open: escape potential/closed: collision and injury potential)

- ceiling fans (injury potential)

- open washing machines, dryers, refrigerators, freezers, ovens or dishwashers (bird flies into, is trapped and forgotten, and dies when appliance is activated)

- open toilet bowls (drowning)

- uncovered fish tanks (drowning)

- leaded stained glass items or inlaid jewelry (poisoning)

- uncovered cooking pots on the stove (drowning/scalding/poisoning/burn potential)

- crayons and permanent markers (poisoning)

- pesticides, rodent killers and snail bait (poisoning)

- untended stove burners (burns)

- candles (burns)

- open trash cans (injury by flying into and possibly being tossed out with the trash)

Parrot-proofing your home is akin to baby-proofing it. If you consider that the average macaw or cockatoo is intellectually and emotionally a perpetual 2-year-old, you'll have some idea of the responsibility parrot owners take on when they adopt their pets. Although your parakeet is smaller than a cockatoo or a macaw, he is no less curious than his larger cousins and no less precious to you than those larger birds are to their owners, so be aware of the potential dangers found in your home.

The dangers don't stop with the furniture and accessories. A plethora of fumes can overpower your pet, too, such as those from cigarettes, air fresheners, insecticides, bleach, shoe polish, oven cleaners, kerosene, lighter fluid, model and instant glues, active self-cleaning ovens, hair spray, overheated nonstick cookware, paint thinner, bathroom cleaners or nail polish remover. Try to keep your pet away from anything that has a strong chemical odor, and be sure to apply makeup and hair care products far away from your parakeet.

To help protect your pet from harmful chemical fumes from cleaning products, consider using "green" alternatives, such as baking soda and vinegar to clear clogged drains, baking soda instead of scouring powder, lemon juice and mineral oil to polish furniture, and white vinegar and water as a window cleaner. Not only will you help your parakeet stay healthy, you'll make the environment healthier, too!

Home remodeling and improvement projects can also cause harm to your pet parakeet. Fumes from paint or formaldehyde, which can be found in carpet backing, paneling and particle board, can cause pets and people to become ill. If you are having work done on your home, consider boarding your parakeet at your avian veterinarian's office or at the home of a bird-loving friend or relative until the project is complete and the house is aired out fully. You can consider the house safe for your pet when you cannot smell any trace of any of the products used in the remodeling.

Another potentially hazardous situation arises when you have your home chemically treated for insects. Ask your exterminator for information about the types of chemicals that will be used in your home, and inquire if pet-safe formulas are available.

BE CAREFUL WITH KISSES

Because saliva poses a health hazard to your parakeet, please don't kiss him on the beak (kiss him on top of his little head instead). Don't allow your parakeet to put his head into your mouth, nibble on your lips or preen your teeth, either. Although you may see birds doing this on television or in pictures in a magazine and think that it's a cute trick, it's very unsafe for your bird's health and well-being.

If you have other pets in the home that require flea treatments, consider pyrethrin-based products. These natural flea killers are derived from chrysanthemums and, although they aren't as long lasting as synthetic substitutes, they do knock down fleas quickly and are safer in the long run for your pets and you. Or you can treat your dog or cat's sleeping area with diatomaceous earth, which is the crushed shells of primitive one-celled algae. This dust kills fleas by mechanical means, which means that fleas will never develop a resistance to it as they could with chemical products.

Other pets can be harmful to your parakeet's health, too. A curious cat could claw or bite your

71

bird, a dog could step on him accidentally or bite him or another, larger bird could break his leg or rip off his upper mandible with his beak. If your parakeet tangles with another pet in your home, contact your avian veterinarian immediately because emergency treatment (for bacterial infection from a puncture wound or shock from being stepped on or suffering a broken bone) may be required to save your parakeet's life.

Owners and other people can unintentionally be a parakeet's worst enemy. You may want to nap

Some illnesses can be caused by common house-hold items like plants, so make sure that yours are not toxic to birds.

with your bird, but you could easily roll over on him while doing so. Another common problem is the danger caused by leaving nonstick cookware on the stove and having it boil dry. In the process, toxic fumes are released that can kill a beloved pet bird.

Moreover, marathon cooking sessions may result in overheated cookware or stovetop drip pans, which could kill your bird if the cookware or drip pans are coated with a nonstick finish. (You may want to consider replacing your nonstick cookware with stainless steel pots and pans or glass cook-ware, which you can treat with a nonstick cooking spray to make cleanups safe and easy.) Similarly, the self-cleaning cycle on some ovens can create harmful fumes for pet birds. Use this cycle only if you've opened the windows around your bird's cage to let in fresh air. (Make sure your parakeet's cage is closed securely before opening a window.)

PARAKEET FIRST AID

Sometimes your pet will get himself into a situation that will require

quick thinking and even quicker action on your part to help save your bird from serious injury or death. Knowledge of some basic first aid techniques may prove useful in these situations.

First and foremost, make sure that you have a bird owner's first aid kit (see sidebar in this chapter for information on what to include).

In *The Complete Bird Owner's Handbook,* veterinarian Gary Gallerstein offers the following advice to bird owners whose birds need urgent care.

No matter what the situation, there are a few things to keep in mind when facing a medical emergency with your pet. First, keep as calm as possible because your bird is already excited enough from being injured, and your getting excited won't help your pet get well. Next, stop any bleeding, keep the bird warm and minimize handling him.

After you've stabilized your pet, call your veterinarian's office for further instructions. Tell them "This is an emergency" and that your bird has had an accident. Describe what happened to your pet as clearly and calmly as you can. Listen carefully to the instructions you are given and follow them. Finally, transport your bird to the vet's office as quickly and safely as you can.

Here are some urgent medical situations that bird owners are likely

Although this kitten looks as if she wouldn't hurt a fly, most cats could prove to be a serious health hazard for birds.

to encounter, the reason that they are medical emergencies, the signs and symptoms your bird might show and the recommended treatments for the problem.

Animal Bites

Infections can develop from bacteria on the biting animal's teeth and/or claws. Also, a bird's internal organs can be damaged by the bite. Sometimes the bite marks can be seen, but often the bird shows few, if any, signs of injury.

Call your veterinarian's office and transport the bird there immediately. Treatment for shock and antibiotics are often the course of action veterinarians take to save birds that have been bitten.

Beak Injury

A bird needs both his upper and lower beak (also called the upper and lower mandible) to eat and preen properly. Infections can set in rather quickly if a beak is fractured or punctured.

An obvious symptom is bleeding from the beak. This often occurs after the bird flies into a windowpane or mirror, or if he has a run-in

with an operational ceiling fan. The beak may also be cracked or damaged, in which case portions of the beak may be missing.

Control bleeding. Keep the bird calm and quiet. Contact your avian veterinarian's office.

Bleeding

A bird can only withstand about a 20 percent loss of blood volume (in a parakeet, about twelve drops) and still recover from an injury. In the event of external bleeding, you will see blood on the bird, his cage and his surroundings. In the case of internal bleeding, the bird may pass bloody droppings or bleed from his nose, mouth or vent.

For external bleeding, apply direct pressure. If the bleeding doesn't stop with direct pressure, apply a coagulant, such as styptic powder (for nails and beaks) or cornstarch (for broken feathers and skin injuries). If the bleeding stops, observe the bird to make sure the bleeding does not resume and the bird does not go into shock. Call your veterinarian's office if the bird seems weak or if he has lost a lot of blood. If you cannot stop the bleeding, arrange to take the bird in for further treatment.

Breathing Problems

Respiratory problems in pet birds can be life threatening. The bird wheezes or clicks while breathing, bobs his tail, breathes with an open mouth and has discharge from his nares or swelling around his eyes.

Keep the bird warm, place him in a bathroom with a hot shower running to help him breathe easier and call your veterinarian's office.

Burns

Birds that are burned severely enough can go into shock and may die. A burned bird has reddened skin and burnt or greasy feathers. The bird may also show signs of shock (see below for details).

Mist the burned area with cool water. Apply antibiotic cream or spray lightly. Do not apply any oily or greasy substances, such as butter. If the bird seems shocky or the burn is widespread, contact your veterinarian's office immediately for further instructions.

SAFE AND POISONOUS PLANTS

Even common houseplants can pose a threat to your pet's health. Here are some plants that are considered **poisonous** to parakeets:

- amaryllis
- calla lily
- daffodil
- dieffenbachia
- English ivy

- foxglove
- holly
- lily-of-the-valley
- mistletoe
- rhubarb

What's a parakeet owner to do? Are there any safe plants that you can keep in your home without endangering your feathered friend? Fortunately, yes, there are.

Some plants that are considered **safe** for bird owners to have in their homes include:

- African violets
- aloe
- burro's tail
- Christmas cactus

- edible fig
- ferns
- gardenia
- grape ivy

Concussion

A concussion results from a sharp blow to the head that can cause injury to the brain. Birds sometimes suffer concussions when they fly into mirrors or windows. They will

FIRST AID KIT

You should assemble a bird owner's first aid kit so that you will have some basic supplies on hand before your bird needs them. Here's what to include:

- appropriate-sized towels for catching and holding your bird
- a heating pad, heat lamp or other heat source
- styptic powder or cornstarch to stop bleeding (use styptic powder on beak and nails only)
- blunt-tipped scissors
- nail clippers and nail file
- needle-nosed pliers to pull broken blood feathers
- blunt-end tweezers
- hydrogen peroxide or other disinfectant solution
- eye irrigation solution
- bandage materials such as gauze squares, masking tape (it doesn't stick to a bird's feathers like adhesive tape does) and gauze rolls
- Pedialyte or other energy supplement
- eye dropper
- penlight

seem stunned and may go into shock.

Keep the bird warm and quiet, prevent him from hurting himself further and watch him carefully. Alert your veterinarian's office to the injury.

Cloacal Prolapse

In this situation the bird's lower intestines, uterus or cloaca is protruding from his or her vent. You will notice pink, red, brown or black tissue protruding from the vent.

Contact your veterinarian's office for immediate follow-up care. Your veterinarian can usually reposition the organs.

Egg Binding

When an egg is bound, it blocks the hen's excretory system and makes it impossible for her to eliminate. Also, eggs can sometimes break inside the hen, which can lead to infection. An egg-bound hen strains to lay an egg unsuccessfully. She becomes fluffed and lethargic, sits on the floor of her cage, may be paralyzed and may have a swollen abdomen.

Keep her warm because this sometimes helps her pass the egg. Put her and her cage into a warm bathroom with a hot shower running to increase the humidity, which may also help her pass the egg. If your bird doesn't improve shortly (within a hour), contact your veterinarian.

Eye Injury

Untreated eye problems may lead to blindness. Symptoms include swollen or pasty eyelids, discharge, cloudy eyeball, and increased rubbing of eye area.

Examine the eye carefully for foreign bodies. Contact your veterinarian for more information.

Fractures

A fracture can cause a bird to go into shock. Depending on the type of fracture, infections can also set in. Birds most often break bones in their legs, so be on the lookout for a bird who is holding one leg at an odd angle or who isn't putting

weight on one leg. Sudden swelling of a leg or wing or a droopy wing can also indicate fractures.

Confine the bird to his cage or a small carrier. Don't handle him unnecessarily. Keep him warm and contact your veterinarian.

Frostbite

A bird could lose toes or feet to frostbite. He could also go into shock and die as a result. You will be able to notice that the frostbitten area is very cold and dry to the touch and is pale in color.

Warm up the damaged tissue gradually in a circulating water bath. Keep the bird warm and contact your veterinarian's office for further instructions.

Inhaled or Ingested Foreign Object

Birds can develop serious respiratory or digestive problems from foreign objects in their bodies. In the case of inhaled items, symptoms include wheezing and other respiratory problems. If you see your bird playing with a small object that you later cannot find, he may have ingested it.

In either event, contact your veterinarian's office immediately.

Lead Poisoning

Birds can die from lead poisoning. A bird with lead poisoning may act depressed or weak. He may be blind, or he may walk in circles at the bottom of his cage. He may regurgitate or pass droppings that resemble tomato juice.

Contact your avian veterinarian immediately. Lead poisoning requires immediate treatment, and the treatment may require

several days or weeks to complete successfully.

Note: Lead poisoning is easily prevented by keeping birds away from common sources of lead in the home. These include stained glass items, leaded paint found in some older homes, fishing weights, drapery weights and parrot toys (some are weighted with lead). One item that won't cause lead poisoning is a lead pencil (which actually contains graphite).

Overheating

High body temperatures can kill a bird. An overheated bird will hold

Any signs of injury to your parakeet's beak, especially bleeding, are good cause for an immediate trip to the veterinarian.

his wings away from his body, open his mouth and roll his tongue in an attempt to cool himself. Birds don't have sweat glands, so they must try to cool their bodies by exposing as much of their skin's surface as they can to moving air. Cool the bird off by putting him in front of a fan (make sure the blades are screened so the bird doesn't injure himself further), by spraying him with cool water or by having him stand in a bowl of cool water. Let the bird drink cool water if he can (if he can't, offer him cool water with an eydropper) and contact your veterinarian.

Poisoning

Poisons can kill a small bird quickly. Poisoned birds may suddenly regurgitate, have diarrhea or bloody droppings and have redness or burns around their mouths. They may also go into convulsions, become paralyzed or go into shock. Put the poison out of your bird's reach. Contact your veterinarian for further instructions. Be prepared to take the poison with you to the vet's office in case he or she needs to contact a poison control center for further information.

Seizures

Seizures can indicate a number of serious conditions, including lead poisoning, infections, nutritional deficiency, heat stroke and epilepsy. The bird may have a seizure that lasts from a few seconds to a minute. Afterward, he seems dazed and may stay on the cage floor for several hours. He may also appear unsteady and not perch.

Keep the bird from hurting himself further by removing everything you can from his cage. Cover the bird's cage with a towel and darken the room to reduce the bird's stress level. Contact your veterinarian's office for further instructions immediately.

Shock

Shock indicates that the bird's circulatory system cannot move the blood supply around the bird's body. This is a serious condition that can lead to death if left untreated. Shocky birds may act depressed, they may breathe rapidly and they may have a fluffed appearance. If your bird displays these signs in conjunction with a recent accident, suspect shock and take appropriate action.

Keep your bird warm and confined, cover his cage and transport him to your veterinarian's office as soon as possible.

EMERGENCY TIPS

Veterinarian Michael Murray recommends that bird owners keep the following tips in mind when facing emergency situations:

KEEP THE BIRD WARM—You can do this by putting the bird in an empty aquarium with a heating pad under the aquarium floor, by putting a heat lamp near the bird's cage or by putting a heating pad set on low under the bird's cage in place of the cage tray. Whatever heat source you choose to use, make sure to keep a close eye on your bird so that he doesn't accidentally burn himself on the pad or lamp or that he doesn't chew on a power cord.

PUT THE BIRD IN A DARK, QUIET ROOM—This helps reduce the bird's stress.

PUT THE BIRD'S FOOD IN LOCATIONS THAT ARE EASY TO REACH—Sick birds need to eat, but they may not be able to reach food in its normal location in the cage. Sometimes birds require hand-feeding to keep their calorie consumption steady.

PROTECT THE BIRD FROM ADDITIONAL INJURY—If the convalescing bird is in a clear-sided aquarium, for example, you may want to put a towel over the glass to keep the bird from flying into it.

CARING FOR OLDER BIRDS

Older pet birds are prone to a number of health problems, including tumors, vision problems, thyroid gland insufficiencies, chlamydiosis and upper respiratory infections.

Tumors

Parakeets can develop tumors as early as age 5, although if a bird passes the age of 7 without developing a tumor, he will probably live out his life tumor-free. If you notice that your pet's breastbone sticks out a little more than it used to or that your bird has difficulty perching, schedule an evaluation with your avian veterinarian; both of these signs indicate possible tumor development. Tumors develop in pet birds most frequently in the nerves off the bird's spine. A tumor in this spot can impair kidney and gonad function, which can put pressure on the nerve that runs into the bird's leg.

Vision Problems

Vision problems can show themselves in several ways. Your pet may no longer be able to judge distances well, or his eyes may appear clouded over. Just as in older people, cataracts can appear in older parakeets.

Thyroid Problems

Thyroid problems occur frequently in older parakeets. These problems result from either a deficiency in the bird's hormonal system or a need for supplemental iodine in the diet. If your parakeet suddenly gains weight and develops fat deposits that resemble tumors, contact your avian veterinarian to have your pet examined.

Although they may not seem to be connected, a thyroid problem may show itself in a longer-than-average molt. If you notice that your

An adequate amount of sleep each day is necessary for your bird's health.

81

parakeet's molting period seems unusually long as he ages, talk to your avian veterinarian. A hormonal supplement may be in order to help keep your bird healthy.

Although older parakeets are far from being delicate "hothouse flowers," owners of an older bird should pay close attention to their pet's diet to ensure that the bird continues to receive a varied diet that is low in fat. The temperature of the room in which the bird is kept during cool weather should also be monitored. Add supplemental heat by using an incandescent bulb covered with a reflector on one end of your bird's cage. This allows a bird to move closer to the heat source if he is cold and away from it if the bird becomes too warm. Make sure that the bulb is far enough away from the cage so that your pet cannot burn himself on the reflector or the bulb.

As your parakeet ages, the need to watch his daily routine becomes even more important, because health problems that are caught early are easier to treat.

WHEN YOUR PARAKEET DIES

Although birds are relatively long-lived pets, eventually the wonderful relationship between bird and owner ends when the bird dies. While no one has an easy time accepting the death of a beloved pet, children may have more difficulty with the loss than adults.

Let your child know that it's okay to feel sad about losing your parakeet. Encourage your child to draw pictures of the bird, to make a collage using photos of your pet parakeet or pictures of parakeets from magazines, to write stories or poems about it or to talk about the loss. Also explain to the child that these sad feelings will pass with time.

While helping their children cope with the death of a pet, parents need to remember that it's okay for adults to feel sad, too. Don't diminish your feelings of loss by telling yourself that "It's only a bird." Pets fill important roles in our lives and our families. Whenever we lose someone close to us, we grieve.

Although you may feel as though you never want another bird because of the pain caused by your parakeet's death, don't let the loss of your parakeet keep you from owning other birds. Discuss bringing home a new pet bird with your family, your avian veterinarian and bird breeders in your area. Together, you can work out a plan that's best for you and your family!

A Matter of Fact

Presently, scientists have identified about 750 parrot species. Of these, some 280 are kept as pets, and about 250 of those have bred successfully in captivity, assuring that parrots will be around for future generations to enjoy. Prospective bird owners will find themselves in good company historically, because birds have been kept as pets for centuries.

BIRD KEEPING THROUGH THE AGES

The ancient Egyptians are credited with being the first to keep birds, most notably pigeons. Queen Hatsheput (1504 to 1482 B.C.) was credited as being the first monarch to create a royal zoo, which included exotic birds. The ancient Persians also knew about talking birds as early as the fifth century B.C., when a court physician and naturalist wrote about talking birds described to him by Indian merchants.

Classical Greece and Rome

From Egypt, bird keeping spread to Greece and Rome. Alexander the Great receives credit from some historians with discovering the Alexandrine parakeet, and the Greeks are credited with popularizing parrot keeping outside of the birds' native lands of Africa and Asia.

Well-to-do Romans built extensive garden aviaries, and they also employed mockingbirds in the entryways of their homes as feathered doorbells to announce visitors. The Romans are thought to have been the first bird dealers, bringing different types of birds to Great Britain and the European continent.

Europe

Until the Renaissance, bird keeping was a hobby that only the wealthy could pursue. After canaries were introduced to Europe by Portuguese sailors, bird keeping grew more popular as a hobby, although it was still confined largely to upper-class fanciers. In the 1600s, the Dutch began producing varieties of canaries for show. These birds were exported to Britain, and bird keeping began

to be more accessible to the masses.

Bird keeping as we know it today can be traced to its beginnings in Victorian Great Britain, when bird sellers in the British Isles would offer goldfinches and larks to ship captains en route to the West Indies. These common European birds would then be traded in the islands for species found there.

THE PARAKEET'S BACKGROUND

You may know parakeets by their formal name, budgerigars. Others may call them budgies. The aboriginally derived term "budgerigar" describes the subject of this book— a single species, *Melopsittacus undulatus,* that constitutes its own genus. In contrast, the term "parakeet" is a general designation for a number of long-tailed psittacine species.

True Australians

Parakeets come from Australia, where they live in large communal flocks. Many wild parakeets are found in central Australia, which is a harsh, arid land. To cope with these extreme conditions, parakeets have adapted to surviving on minimal food and water requirements. (Notice that the phrase used is surviving, and not thriving. Parakeets kept in captivity need more than seeds and water to thrive.)

The name budgerigar is said to come from an Aboriginal phrase that means "good to eat," although it is hard to imagine eating such personable little birds. The species' scientific name, *Melopsittacus undulatus*, literally means "song parrot with wavy lines," which refers to the birds' melodic voices and the wavy bars across their backs and wings. These wavy lines help wild parakeets camouflage themselves in the Australian grasslands so they are less obvious to predators. In the past, parakeets were also called shell parrots, warbling grass parakeets and zebra parrots.

The Parakeet Arrives in Europe

The British naturalist John Gould is credited with bringing the parakeet to the attention of the pet-loving public. In 1838, Gould and his wife, Elizabeth, traveled from London to Australia to study the continent's native wildlife for a series of books

that Gould was writing. Although he considered parakeets rather dull in personality, Gould brought a pair back to England.

Parakeets soon became popular pets with upper-class Europeans, and hundreds of thousands of them were sent on weeklong sea voyages from Australia to England, Belgium and Holland. Although many birds died in transit, those that survived proved to be surprisingly easy to breed in captivity (Gould's brother-in-law, Charles Coxen, bred the first pair in England in the 1840s), and they were soon being bred across Europe

Bird keeping has its origins in Victorian Great Britain.

The wavy lines on a parakeet's back originated from the species' need for camouflage in the Australian grasslands.

began their current reign of popularity in the United States in the 1950s. Today, about 16 million pet birds are kept in American homes, and 45 percent of them are parakeets, according to statistics from the American Pet Product Manufacturers Association. They are the most popularly kept pet parrot in the world, with some 5 million pet and show birds in Great Britain alone.

ENGLISH AND AMERICAN PARAKEETS

In your search for the perfect pet parakeet, you may have noticed that there are two types of parakeets: the English and the American. The differences between the two birds are slight but noticeable. Parakeet breeder Penny Corbett, in her "Ask the Experts" column in *Bird Talk,* describes the differences as follows: "English budgie breeders concentrate their efforts toward breeding a larger, more majestic bird. Budgie competition is much more widespread in England than it is in the United States. Exhibitors in England have spent more time breeding exhibition budgies, and

by zoological gardens and aristocratic bird keepers.

Birds were still being exported by the thousands from Australia to Europe, South Africa, South America and the United States. Australia finally banned export of parakeets in 1894, a ban that is still in place.

Parakeets in America

Although they have been kept as pets in America for years, parakeets some believe this is how exhibition (or English) budgies got their name.

"American budgies are generally regarded as pet birds," Corbett continues. "They are more active than the mellow English birds, and are often bred in large quantities to supply the demand of the pet trade. The American budgie is generally more outgoing, active and mischievous than its counterpart."

So Why Is the Parakeet So Popular?

Some of the reasons bird lovers are attracted to parakeets include their manageable size, their gentleness, their nondestructiveness, the ease with which they can be handled and tamed, their sociable nature and their talking ability, although the last shouldn't be the sole reason for choosing a parakeet or any other pet bird.

A parakeet's size makes her an easily handled pet for bird lovers, young or old. A healthy parakeet measures about 7 inches from the top of her head to the tip of her tail and weighs about 30 grams (1.05 ounces). This small size comes with a quiet, pleasant voice and a manageable beak.

Because parakeets have been kept as pets for so many years, some people consider them one of the few domesticated pet birds. They seem to enjoy people and being part of an active family. They also seem to want to please their owners by learning tricks or learning to talk, although there is no guarantee that your parakeet will be a trickster or a talker. People choose a parakeet as a pet because they want to share their homes with a bird and appreciate her for the unique being that she is.

PARROT TRAITS

The parakeet is a species of parrot, just like the Hyacinth Macaw or Mealy Amazon. The traits that all parrot species have in common include the following:

- four toes—two pointing backward and two pointing forward
- upper beak overhanging the lower
- broad head and short neck

However, a healthy parakeet measures about 7 inches from tip of the head to tip of the tail, while a full-grown Scarlet Macaw can easily reach 40 inches in length.

Resources

For more information on bird care, look for these books at your local library, bookstore or pet store:

Alderton, David, with illustrations by Graeme Stevenson. *Atlas of Parrots of the World*. Neptune, N.J.: TFH Publications Inc., 1991.

———. *Birdkeeper's Guide to Budgies*. Tetra Press, 1988.

———. *Birdkeeper's Guide to Parrots and Macaws*. Tetra Press, 1989.

———. *You and Your Pet Bird*. New York: Alfred A. Knopf, 1994.

Birmelin, Immanuel, and Annette Wolter. *The New Parakeet Handbook*. Hauppauge, NY: Barron's Educational Series Inc., 1986.

Gallerstein, Gary A. DVM. *The Complete Bird Owner's Handbook*. New York: Howell Book House, 1994.

MAGAZINES

Bird Talk
Monthly magazine devoted to pet bird ownership. Subscription information: 2401 Beverly Blvd., P.O. Box 57900, Los Angeles, CA 90057.

Birds USA
Annual magazine aimed at first-time bird owners. Subscription information:
2401 Beverly Blvd., P.O. Box 57900, Los Angeles, CA 90057.

Caged Bird Hobbyist
This magazine for pet bird owners is published seven times a year.
Subscription information: 7-L Dundas Circle, Greensboro, NC 27407.

Parakeets YearBOOK
Published by yearBOOKS Inc., 1 TFH Plaza, Neptune, NJ 07753. Look for
it in your local pet store or bookstore.

ON-LINE RESOURCES

Bird Breeder
On-line magazine dedicated to the concerns of bird breeders who raise and
sell pet birds. www.birdbreeder.com.

89

In addition to *Bird Breeder*, bird-specific sites have been cropping
up regularly on the Internet. These sites offer pet bird owners the opportunity to share stories about their pets and trade helpful hints about bird
care.

If you belong to an on-line service, look for the pet site (it's sometimes
included in more general topics, such as "Hobbies and Interests," or more
specifically "Pets"). If you have Internet access, use your Web browser or
WebCrawler to search for "parrots" or "pet birds."

BIRD CLUBS

AMERICAN BUDGERIGAR SOCIETY
1704 Kangaroo
Killeen, TX 76543

THE AMERICAN FEDERATION OF AVICULTURE
P.O. Box 56218
Phoenix, AZ 85079-6128

AVICULTURAL SOCIETY OF AMERICA
P.O. Box 5516
Riverside, CA 92517-5517

INTERNATIONAL AVICULTURAL SOCIETY
P.O. Box 280383
Memphis, TN 38168

SOCIETY OF PARROT BREEDERS AND EXHIBITORS
P.O. Box 369
Groton, MA 01450